THE PREHISTORY OF LANGUAGES

# JANUA LINGUARUM

## STUDIA MEMORIAE
## NICOLAI VAN WIJK DEDICATA

*edenda curat*

C. H. VAN SCHOONEVELD

INDIANA UNIVERSITY

SERIES MINOR

NR. 57

MOUTON

THE HAGUE · PARIS

# THE PREHISTORY
# OF LANGUAGES

*by*

MARY R. HAAS

UNIVERSITY OF CALIFORNIA, BERKELEY

MOUTON

THE HAGUE · PARIS

ISBN 90 279 0681 5
© Copyright 1969 in The Netherlands.
Mouton & Co. N.V., Publishers, The Hague.

*First printing 1969*
*Second printing 1978*


LIBRARY OF CONGRESS CATALOG CARD NUMBER 76-75689


Printed in The Netherlands by Mouton & Co., Printers, The Hague.

PREFACE

Most of the present work was published originally under the title "Historical Linguistics and the Genetic Relationship of Languages" and appeared in *Current Trends in Linguistics*, Vol. III, ed. by Thomas A. Sebeok (1966). In presenting this material as a separate publication in the Series minor of *Janua Linguarum*, a shorter title, *The Prehistory of Languages*, has been chosen, and a number of changes, both by way of addition and of deletion, have been introduced. Deletions are not extensive except in Chapter 4. Chapter 5 is entirely new. The Appendix contains a paper which belongs with the general thinking that went into the preparation of this volume but properly stands somewhat apart. A bibliography has also been added.

The freedom from normal academic routine which has been provided during 1967-68 has made it possible to carry forward my studies in the linguistic prehistory of North America and, as a byproduct, to revise and expand my earlier paper into its present form. As a Senior Fellow of the National Endowment for the Arts and Humanities and concurrently as a Fellow in residence at the Center for Advanced Study in the Behavioral Sciences, I am happy to express my deep gratitude to both organizations for this op- portunity.

Mary R. Haas

*Stanford, California*
May, 1968

# TABLE OF CONTENTS

# LIST OF TABLES

# 1. INTRODUCTION

## 1.1 THE PREHISTORY OF LANGUAGES
## VS. THE PREHISTORY OF LANGUAGE

The 'prehistory of languages' is not to be confused with a different topic which might be called the 'prehistory of language'. Among other things, the latter would inevitably involve us in the problem of the origin of language. While this is a topic which is once more receiving serious consideration after being under a cloud for over a century, it is not the problem concerning us here. Moreover, recent discoveries make it clear that man evolved nearly two million years ago. This means that language may very well have been slowly evolving over hundreds of thousands of years. It is therefore no longer necessary to think of it as something which arose a few thousand years ago, as was widely believed not so long ago. In fact it is no longer seriously to be argued that language preceded even the lowliest forms of material culture. On the contrary, there is a growing body of evidence to indicate that brain development was triggered by tool-use and this in turn was a necessary concomitant in the acquisition of language.

Our concern here, however, is with what may be called the 'prehistory of languages', a topic which might be thought of as a kind of 'linguistic archeology'. This is a matter in regard to which we have, over the course of the past 150 years, developed a quite explicit methodology. Through the proper use of this methodology the linguist is able to arrive at, to 'reconstruct', a considerable amount of quite precise information about a language of the past provided he has good information about the various descendants of that language (and provided of course that the language has more than one descendant with which to work). The usual technical term for this method is simply the 'comparative method' and the usual technical term for what can be reconstructed of the ancestor language is 'protolanguage'. Such a protolanguage may have been spoken from one to several thousands of years ago.

The nineteenth century is celebrated in the history of linguistics because of its development of the comparative method and its successful application of the method to that family of languages known as Indo-European which comprises many of the languages of India and most of the languages of Europe. The method has also been applied with great success to several branches of the Indo-European family, such as Romance, Germanic, and Slavic.

### 1.2 REGULARITY OF SOUND CHANGE

The most important breakthrough in the development of the comparative method came when it was discovered that, among languages which are related to one another, it is possible to work out a series of statements about the sounds of these languages such that every $x$ in language A corresponds to $y$ in language B and to $z$ in language C. (This subincludes the possibilities that $y$ and $z$ are identical with $x$, that $y$ or $z$ is identical with $x$, and that $y$ is identical with $z$ but not with $x$). This principle, which came to be known as 'the regularity of sound change', is one of the truly great discoveries in the history of linguistics.

The importance of this discovery was far-reaching. For, as Bloomfield emphasized in a late essay,[1]

... a new mastery of historical perspective brought about, at the beginning of the nineteenth century, the development of comparative and historical linguistics. The method of this study may fairly be called one of the triumphs of nineteenth century *science*. In a survey of *scientific method it should serve as a model* of one type of investigation, since *no other historical discipline has equalled it*. (p. 2) [Emphasis mine.]

[1] Leonard Bloomfield, "Linguistic aspects of science", *Foundations of the unity of science*, 1.4.1-59 (1939).

Indeed the very term 'linguistic science', so commonly used in this period, seems more often than not to have meant 'historical and comparative linguistics'. Moreover, the discipline was generally acknowledged to be the most rigorous and hence most 'scientific' of all those branches of knowledge commonly subsumed under such terms as the humanities and the social sciences, or, as Sapir[2] has pointed out: "In the course of their detailed researches Indo-European linguists have gradually developed a technique which is *more nearly perfect than that of any other science dealing with man's institutions.*" (p. 207) [Emphasis mine.] In that same period anthropology, for example, was struggling to achieve the status of a scientific discipline, whereas linguistics, even though being claimed as a branch of anthropology,[3] had already achieved recognition as a scientific discipline of the highest order. The success of linguistics thus served as a spur to many other disciplines, particularly those concerned with 'man's institutions'.

What was it that linguistics had that other disciplines sought to emulate? Clyde Kluckhohn[4] has expressed it this way:

In a period when even some natural scientists considered the systematic study of humanity as fruitless because of the complexities involved or actually denounced it as contravening the conception of God-given free will, *the success of comparative philology,* perhaps more than any other single fact, *encouraged students of man to seek for regularities in human behavior* (p. 110) [Emphasis mine.]

---

[2]  Edward Sapir, "The status of linguistics as a science", *Lg.*, 5.207-14 (1929).
[3]  The latter part of the nineteenth century was characterized by an almost feverish desire to classify everything, including scientific disciplines which were subdivided into a variety of branches and subbranches. Among many others, Daniel G. Brinton proposed a scheme 'for the nomenclature and classification of the anthropological sciences' which included four main branches: 'I. *Somatology*: Physical and Experimental Anthropology'; 'II. *Ethnology*: Historic and Analytic Anthropology'; 'III. *Ethnography*: Geographic and Descriptive Anthropology'; and 'IV. *Archeology*: Prehistoric and Reconstructive Anthropology'. 'Linguistics' finds its place as item (e) under *Ethnology*. See Daniel G. Brinton, "The nomenclature and teaching of anthropology", *American Anthropologist*, o.s., 5.263-71 (1892), particularly pp. 265-6.
[4]  Clyde Kluckhohn, "Patterning as exemplified in Navaho culture", *Language, culture and personality*, eds. Leslie Spier, A. Irving Hallowell, and Stanley S. Newman 110 (Menasha, Wisconsin, 1941).

Linguistics had a rigorous method of demonstrating the genetic relationship of languages. Moreover, it had amassed a great amount of material that was more than sufficient to prove the genetic relationship of what is now known as the Indo-European family of languages. The key to success in this demonstration can be summed up in two simple statements:

(1) Phonetic 'laws'[5] are regular provided it is recognized that

(2) certain seemingly aberrant forms can be shown to be the results of analogy or borrowing.

The discovery of these truths was crucial in establishing linguistics as a scientific discipline. Though they may seem simple enough now — as all great truths do, once they are formulated — they did not take form overnight and they were not arrived at without many a false start and wrong assumption. Moreover — and this may come as a surprise to many — their power has not yet been fully exploited. There are dozens and dozens of linguistic families in the world but few indeed can lay claim to having been as thoroughly studied and as adequately reconstructed as Indo-European.[6] If we can convince ourselves of the necessity of applying the rigorous methodology already developed for Indo-European to as many other families as possible, we can hope to achieve many highly rewarding advances in our knowledge of farflung genetic relationships among the languages of the world. But if we are unable to convince ourselves of this necessity, our handbooks will continue to be filled with highly speculative and all too often plainly dubious or misleading information.

[5] The term 'law' is a misnomer if interpreted as a universal term. A 'phonetic law' simply states what phone is found in a particular language at a particular time in terms of its correspondent in an earlier language (attested in writing or reconstructed), or vice versa.

[6] This is not, of course, intended to imply that the work on Indo-European is now complete. On the contrary, a reassessment is urgently needed in order to integrate the vast amount of new material that has become available to scholars in the twentieth century.

## 1.3 OBSTACLES TO BROADER APPLICATIONS

Because of the remarkable success achieved by nineteenth century linguists in the reconstruction of Proto Indo-European, it might have been expected that linguists would not rest until they had succeeded in working out the prehistory of as many language families of the world as possible. The vastness of the wealth of information waiting to be recovered by these means staggers the imagination. But things did not quite turn out this way. There were two compelling reasons for this, one trivial (though not vanquished without the spilling of a great quantity of ink) and the other practical.

Some of the greatest discoveries about the probable nature of Proto Indo-European were made on the basis of written documents in languages, such as Latin, Greek, and Sanskrit, which had been dead for two or three thousand years. Scholars found these long-dead languages to be so important for them — and in this they were right — that they made the further assumption that the prehistory of languages having no written records could never be worked out— and in this they were wrong. The very strong bias against the study of unwritten, or 'preliterate', languages served as an almost unbelievably strong deterrent against the full exploitation of the comparative method on a global basis. This has been the trivial obstacle.

The practical deterrent has been (and still is) the lack of materials on hundreds of unwritten languages still spoken today and many others still spoken until quite recently. The latter, of course, can never be recovered, but the overcoming of the lack of materials on the others, even on a small scale, turned out to be a much more complicated and involved process than even those most strongly favoring it could have expected. It led, among other things, to the underemphasis of historical studies of the type which had dominated nineteenth century linguistics, and to the over-emphasis of what came to be called descriptive or synchronic studies.

The development of adequate techniques for writing down and

describing spoken languages (literary and nonliterary alike) came to be an end in itself and it engaged the talents of some of our best linguists for decades. While interest in the historical and comparative study of languages did not die out completely, it suffered considerable neglect during the first half of the twentieth century while the predominant concern was with the development of rigorous techniques for synchronic analysis. But the tide is turning again as we are now approaching the last quarter of the twentieth century and there is a steadily increasing interest in the historical and comparative study of languages, particularly of those unwritten languages on which we are at last beginning to amass enough material to do the job. More and more younger scholars in particular, are turning their attention to the rewarding task of reconstructing protolanguages, and we are gradually accumulating a respectable body of material giving us remarkably good information about undocumented languages spoken from two to four or five thousand years ago. Such work is moving forward not only in respect to the aboriginal languages of North and South America, but of Asia, Africa, and Australia as well. The 'impossibility' of the latter part of the nineteenth century bids fair to become the outstanding accomplishment of the latter part of the twentieth century.

## 1.4 WRITTEN AND UNWRITTEN LANGUAGES

Although scholars in the eighteenth century were already fumbling with notions of language relationship, their efforts were on the whole crude. It was not until Sanskrit became known to scholars of the West that real progress began to be made. Sanskrit was much older than the oldest languages of Europe then known, and it had, moreover, its own grammarians, the study of whose work helped provide answers to problems that had previously vexed scholars. Nevertheless, even this great treasure house did not provide ready-made solutions to all problems. The proper evaluation and interpretation of the material was acquired only gradually. For example, it was thought at first that since Sanskrit was older than other then known Indo-European languages everything about it was to be considered a more accurate reflection of an earlier state of affairs than anything found in more recent languages. Scholars tended to feel that if Sanskrit was not itself the 'ancestor' of Greek, Latin and most other languages of Europe, it was nonetheless chronologically so much closer to it that its testimony should take precedence over the testimony of the younger languages.[7] The numerous errors that were engendered by this approach were eventually corrected, however, and this in itself was one of the triumphs of Indo-European scholarship. That much the same kinds of problems had to be tackled all over again with the discovery of the still older Hittite in the early part of the twentieth century means only that it takes time to assess the evidence from a previously unknown cognate language and that chronological readjustments are not easy to make on short notice.

Today it is commonplace for students to take 'field methods' courses and it is taken for granted that a well-trained student will be able to cope with any language in the world whether or not it has ever been written down. Indeed, one of the most beneficial aspects of modern applied linguistics is the devising of alphabets for unwritten languages as an aid in combatting illiteracy. In view of our present sophistication in this regard, it is hard to realize how enslaved the minds of scholars of only a few decades ago were to writing and to the written forms of language. It comes as something of a shock to realize that most of the great advances in Indo-European studies were made under the illusion that the written language was *the* language. The rationale of this unquestioned

---

[7] William Dwight Whitney, in an article originally published in 1867, eloquently expresses the situation in the following words: "The temptation is well-nigh irresistible to set up unduly as an infallible norm a language [Sanskrit] which casts so much light and explains so many difficulties; to exaggerate all its merits and overlook its defects; to defer to its authority in cases where it does not apply; to accept as of universal value its features of local and special growth; to treat it, in short, as if it were the *mother* of the Indo-European dialects, instead of the *eldest sister* in the family." [Emphasis mine.] See Whitney, "Indo-European philology and ethnology", *Oriental and linguistic studies*, 1.198-238 (New York, 1874), pp. 203-4. Of course Sanskrit can no longer even be considered the 'eldest sister'.

assumption is not hard to find. The fact that Sanskrit, for example, was a written language is the reason that we know it well today. If it had not been written we should certainly never be able to know what we do know about it. Even with all our hard-earned skill in the reconstruction of protolanguages, we would not quite be able to 'reconstruct' Sanskrit by comparing the modern Indic vernaculars. So even though we are no longer dependent upon the discovery of written documents in advancing our knowledge of linguistic relationship (in the case of unwritten languages, for example), it would be a serious mistake not to recognize the great value of written languages. In particular there is the historical consideration that we might never have arrived at the point of being able to reconstruct great numbers of the morphs of an unwritten language we call Proto-Indo-European if we had not had written documents of many Indo-European languages at different time levels to help us verify our results and thus give us confidence in our methods. With written languages of different time levels scholars can check their hypotheses in two directions because they have documented verification which provides relative chronology. Scholars who work with unwritten languages cannot do this in quite the same way since they have only one DOCUMENTED time-point, namely the present.

But the earlier reliance on written languages needs to be noted in order to see how it eventually threatened to become an impediment to the further development of linguistic science. Since the existence of written languages, particularly those long extinct whose age can be calculated not only in centuries but millennia, was of great strategic importance in the development of our knowledge of Indo-European, some scholars came to believe that the historical and comparative study of languages was impossible without written records of earlier stages of the same or related languages.

Before this view could be refuted, a clear demonstration of its fallacy would be needed. Leonard Bloomfield determined to provide such a demonstration and this gave rise to an important chapter in the development of comparative linguistics.

## 1.5  COMPARING UNWRITTEN LANGUAGES

Bloomfield, usually celebrated for the prominent role he played in the development of DESCRIPTIVE (as opposed to historical) linguistics after 1933, the year his book *Language* appeared, was actually one of the greatest historical linguists of this century. A fine Germanic and Indo-European scholar, he also became interested in the Algonkian languages of North America and soon recognized the feasibility of reconstructing Proto-Algonkian. That the task imposed problems and difficulties of a type not likely to be encountered by the Indo-European comparativist made it all the more intriguing.

The Algonkian languages were of course not 'written' languages in the ordinary sense of the term, and of course there were no written records of any earlier stages of any of the languages. On the other hand, many of them had been written down, in one fashion or another, by nonnatives of several nationalities, particularly missionaries and travelers, and there was a far greater amount of material in existence on these languages than on any other language family of North America.[8] Brief vocabularies and other materials on one or another Algonkian form of speech began appearing as early as 1609,[9] and by 1663 Eliot had completed his monumental task of translating the Bible into Natick (or Massachusetts).[10] A few years later Eliot published *The Indian grammar begun, or an essay to bring the Indian language into rules*,[11] but this language was unfortunately one of those which became extinct before modern firsthand studies could be made of it.

From these beginnings the stream of materials on Algonkian

---

[8]  The remarkable *Bibliography of the Algonquian languages* by James C. Pilling (Washington, 1891) is by far the largest (614 pages) of the several bibliographies of important American Indian linguistic families compiled by the same author.
[9]  Fide Pilling, *op. cit.*, p. 577. According to this source the earliest material published was a list of numerals of Souriquois, or Etchemin, which appeared in *Histoire de la novelle France contenant les navigations, découvertes, et habitations faites par les François ...*, by Marc Lescarbot (Paris, 1609).
[10]  John Eliot, *The holy Bible, containing the Old Testament and the New* (Cambridge, 1663).
[11]  Cambridge, 1666.

languages became a virtual flood. There were many dictionaries, some bilingual for French, English, or German, some for more than one of these. There were grammars[12] and etymological studies and numerous other works. Moreover, the resemblances among the languages were such that it had long been recognized that they were genetically related and that this remarkable family had a geographical spread greater than that of any other family in North America. So there were even scholars who had commenced comparative work on these languages, the most notable of whom was Truman Michelson,[13] but the results, though considerable, had been only haphazardly presented when Bloomfield entered the field. In order to give a rigorous demonstration of the genetic relationship of these languages, it was obvious to Bloomfield that he would have to reconstruct the protolanguage, and he proposed to do so by using exactly the same techniques that had been so successfully applied by the neogrammarians in the reconstruction of Proto-Indo-European.[14] Furthermore, since many Indo-European scholars thought such a task could not be successfully accomplished in the absence of written records of earlier stages of the languages, Bloomfield set out quite deliberately to disprove this thesis. The result was his masterly paper "On the sound-system of Central Algon-

[12] One of the most famous of these is a nineteenth century one, *A grammar of the Cree language, with which is combined an analysis of the Chippeway dialect*, by Joseph Howse (London, 1844). The most recent grammar is Bloomfield's own study of Menomini, never entirely completed and published posthumously: *The Menomini language* (New Haven-London, 1962).
[13] His first important work on Algonkian was "Preliminary report on the linguistic classification of Algonquian tribes", *Annual Report of the Bureau of [American] Ethnology, 1906-07*, 221-90b (Washington, 1912). Many others followed since the study of these languages remained his principal preoccupation throughout his life. Sapir and Kroeber also made early contributions to the study of comparative Algonkian, e.g. Edward Sapir, "Algonkin *p* and *s* in Cheyenne", *American Anthropologist*, n.s., 15.538-9 (1913); A. L. Kroeber, "Arapaho dialects", *Univ. of Calif. Public. in Amer. Arch. and Ethn.*, 12.3.71-138 (1916), especially pp. 77-80.
[14] Holger Pedersen, *The discovery of language (Linguistic science in the nineteenth century)*, 277-310 (Bloomington, 1962). This is a reprinting of John W. Spargo's translation (Cambridge, 1931).

quian"[15] which paved the way for all future work in comparative Algonkian. To make sure that the nature of his accomplishment, with its important implications for similar work on all unwritten languages, would not be lost on his Indo-European confreres in Europe, he appended the following footnote:

I hope, also, to help dispose of the notion that the usual processes of linguistic change are suspended on the American continent. (Meillet and Cohen, *Les langues du monde*, Paris, 1924, p. 9). If there exists anywhere a language in which these processes do not occur (sound-change independent of meaning, analogic change, etc.), then they will not explain the history of Indo-European or any other language. A principle such as the regularity of phonetic change is not part of the specific tradition handed on to each new speaker of a given language, but is either a universal trait of human speech or nothing at all, an error. (p. 130).

### 1.6 BLOOMFIELD'S ALGONKIAN DEMONSTRATION

Bloomfield's success is reconstructing Proto-Algonkian is of great significance in demonstrating that the principles of historical linguistics can be applied to unwritten languages. He started out with the intention of showing that the 'sounds' of the protolanguage of a set of unwritten related languages could be reconstructed with the same degree of rigor and reliability as had been achieved for the Indo-European languages. Before he could do this, however, he saw that he would have to have a completely accurate and reliable 'description' of each unwritten language that was to be used in the demonstration. All too frequently nonnatively written materials were entirely inadequate for his purposes.[16] In order to achieve the utmost rigor in his demonstration he considered it necessary to maintain a scrupulous distinction between descriptive linguistics

---

[15]  *Lg.*, 1.130-56 (1925).
[16]  However, he used such materials when he had no other choice. For example, in the paper just cited he says: "... for Cree I use Lacombe, *Dictionnaire et grammaire de la langue des Cris* (Montreal 1874), correcting the forms where necessary, from observations made last summer for the Canadian Bureau of Mines" (130). Later on, when he had more materials of his own on Cree, he relied most heavily on these.

and historical linguistics.[17] Perhaps the clearest statement of his position is to be found in the following oft-quoted passage:[18]

All historical study of language is based upon the comparison of two or more sets of descriptive data. It can be only as accurate and only as complete as these data permit it to be. In order to describe a language one needs no historical knowledge whatever; in fact, the observer who allows such knowledge to affect his description, is bound to distort his data. Our descriptions must be unprejudiced [by history], if they are to give a sound basis for comparative study.

This is a strong statement and it was carried to extremes by some of his successors. Bloomfield could not foresee that a completely ahistorical bias (such as became dominant in the 1940s and 1950s) might also lead to a distortion of data.

But in the context of its time the statement was needed. We sêe here that the development of a rigorous methodology in comparative linguistics in the nineteenth century led to the development of a rigorous methodology of descriptive linguistics in the twentieth century. It was precisely because Bloomfield was deeply concerned with reconstructing the phonological and grammatical structure of Proto-Algonkian that caused him to urge the necessity of first having adequate descriptions of the languages to be used in making the reconstruction. This was no idle or sterile conviction. It culminated in the tightly-knit paper entitled simply "Algonquian", ostensibly the only comparative sketch in *Linguistic Structures of Native America*,[19] but actually an outline descriptive grammar of the protolanguage.

The greatness of Bloomfield's treatment of Algonkian can be ascribed to a variety of reasons.[20] A very important point of

[17]   It is well known, of course, that Bloomfield was not the first champion of this position. Another great historical linguist, Ferdinand de Saussure had earlier described the distinction in terms of synchronic and diachronic linguistics; *Cours de linguistique générale* (1916).
[18]   Leonard Bloomfield, *Language*, pp. 19-20.
[19]   By Harry Hoijer and others (= *Viking Fund Publications in Anthropology*, 6) (New York, 1946).
[20]   Some of these reasons are set forth in an appreciation of Bloomfield's work on Algonkian written some years ago by C. F. Hockett; see "Implications of Bloomfield's Algonquian studies", *Lg.*, 24.117-38 (1948) (reprinted in *Readings in Linguistics*, ed. Martin Joos 281-289, Washington, D.C., 1957).

methodology lies in his LIMITATION OF THE PROBLEM to the comparison of four languages[21] for which he had adequate (though often less than abundant) descriptive materials, namely Fox, Cree, Menomini, and Ojibwa. This method had both advantages and disadvantages, though for an INITIAL comprehensive statement of Algonkian comparative grammar the advantages seem far to outweigh the disadvantages. The languages chosen are all so-called Central languages and do not comprise even these in toto. To have attempted to use all available materials on the dozens of Algonkian languages for which some kind of information was available[22] would have rendered the task so unwieldy and unmanageable that he would not have been able to complete it in a lifetime. By limiting himself to those languages over which he had good control he was able (1) to work out the phonological system for Proto-Algonkian as reflected in those particular four Central languages, and (2) to reconstruct large numbers of fully inflected words rather than being confined solely to the reconstruction of roots.[23] The second result had the further advantage of enabling him to write the outline descriptive grammar of the protolanguage mentioned above. He had also begun work on a comparative dictionary of his four selected Algonkian languages, and to this end had assembled extensive slip files on each of them. He did not live to complete the task himself but progress toward achieving this goal is now being made by other scholars.[24]

[21] Otto Dempwolff, working at about the same time on comparative Austronesian, also effectively limited his problem. The principal languages used in his *Vergleichende Lautlehre des Austronesischen Wortschatzes* (Hamburg, 1934) are Javanese, Toba-Batak, and Tagalog.

[22] Pilling's 614-page bibliography of these languages, already referred to, was published in 1891. In the half century following the Pilling publication a great deal more material had been printed on these languages.

[23] It is interesting to observe that, for reasons extraneous to the present discussion, the work on Indo-European led to the reconstruction of roots. This led at least one famous American linguist of the nineteenth century, William Dwight Whitney, to assume that the protolanguage had no inflection; see *Language and the study of language*[5] (New York, 1875), especially pp. 357 and 279.

[24] C. F. Hockett, "Central Algonquian vocabulary: stems in /k-/", *IJAL*, 23.247-68 (1957).

1.7 GENEALOGICAL VS. TYPOLOGICAL CLASSIFICATION

It would be a great satisfaction to be able to say that the work of
Bloomfield on Algonkian, together with that of Sapir on Uto-
Aztecan,[25] Athapaskan,[26] and other linguistic families, not to speak
of the vast amount of work currently being done on the reconstruction and classification of unwritten languages, has succeeded
in allaying the doubts of all Indo-Europeanists about the type of
results that can be achieved without the aid of documentary materials from earlier periods when these are by definition unobtainable.
But in a recent textbook on historical linguistics we find that the old
prejudices, though slightly modified perhaps, have not been entirely
banished. The following quotation, for example, has a familiar
ring:[27]

Genealogical classification was admirably suited to determine the interrelationships of languages such as the Indo-European for which we have
many records from several millennia. For languages attested only today
we may be limited to classification based on typology (p. 49).

Typological classifications are of value in their own right, and can,
needless to say, be applied to anciently recorded languages as well
as to 'languages attested only today'. To imply that genealogical
classification is possible only for linguistic families having written
records of varying chronology while typological classification
belongs to contemporary languages is to sell both types of classification short. Languages are languages, whether written or unwritten, living or dead, and whatever type of classification can be
applied to one can also be applied to any other. The best answer,

[25] Edward Sapir, "Southern Paiute and Nahuatl, a study in Uto-Aztekan", Pt. I
and Pt. II, *Journal de la Société des Américanistes de Paris*, n.s., 10.379-425
(1913) and 11.443-88 (1914).
[26] A discussion of some of his results in comparing the Athapaskan languages
is included by Sapir in "The concept of phonetic law as tested in primitive
languages by Leonard Bloomfield", 297-306 in *Methods in social science: a case
book*, ed. Stuart A. Rice (Chicago, 1931); reprinted 73-82 in *Selected writings of
Edward Sapir*, ed. David G. Mandelbaum (Berkeley-Los Angeles, 1949).
[27] Winfred P. Lehmann, *Historical linguistics* (New York, 1962).

I think, is to paraphrase a statement of Sapir's[28] about the discovery of phonetic laws in unwritten languages:

If these laws are more difficult to discover in primitive [unwritten] languages, this is not due to any special characteristic which these languages possess but merely to the inadequate technique of some who have tried to study them. (p. 74).

In the same way, if genealogical classification is more difficult of achievement in unwritten languages, this is again due to the *'inadequate technique* of some who have tried to study them' [Emphasis mine.] Indeed we might better paraphrase Bloomfield's famous footnote, quoted earlier, and say that the possibility of both genealogical and typological classification 'is either a *universal trait of human speech* or nothing at all, an error' [Emphasis mine.]

There is also still current an even more flagrant misunderstanding of the nature of unwritten languages. Although the error has been refuted innumerable times in the literature, there are still some who believe that unwritten languages change with a rapidity that soon renders reconstruction so tenuous as to be meaningless. A recently expressed version[29] of this view is seen in the following fantastic statement:

In some linguistic families, notably Amerindian and African, *prehistory is but a few decades distant.* Any thrust into the past will involve the linguist in reconstruction... . By the time the Amerindian or African linguist has reached, speaking in terms of the genealogical tree ..., the third or fourth generation, which perhaps carries him backward *no farther than a century* [!], he faces a proto-language of his own making that has an exceedingly small degree of verisimilitude... (p. 32) [Emphasis mine.]

Indeed one might almost say, would that it WERE true! For if among American Indian and African linguistic families, prehistory were 'but a few decades distant', comparative linguists would have a field day. They could take a large 'live' sample every ten years and thus have an actual check on linguistic change that would bid fair to equal the short-lived fruit fly in studying genetic change in

[28] "The concept of phonetic law ...", 74 (of reprint).
[29] Ernst Pulgram, "The nature and use of proto-languages", *Lingua*, 10.18-37 (1961).

biology. Unfortunately for the prospects of any such check, languages change in much the same ways the world over, and writing per se neither retards nor accelerates the change.[30] When sister languages, both written and unwritten, are seen again and again to

[30] This is not to be taken to imply that change in language is never retarded or accelerated; rather it is claimed that (1) writing in itself is NOT NECESSARILY accompanied by significant retardation and, conversely, (2) lack of writing in itself is NOT NECESSARILY accompanied by great acceleration. The study of the possible retardation of replacement of items in the lexicon (especially the so-called 'basic list') is receiving some attention from persons interested in glottochronology (e.g., A. Richard Diebold, Jr., "A control case for glottochronology", *American Anthropologist*, n.s., 66.987-1006 [1964]). An important paper describing one type of condition that could accompany conservatism in lexical replacement is Charles A. Ferguson's "Diglossia", *Word*, 5.325-40 (1959) (reprinted in *Language in culture and society*, ed. Dell Hymes 429-39, New York, Evanston, and London, 1964). He discusses the not uncommon situation in which a superposed or 'high' (H) variety of a language is used, especially by adults, in addition to the regional or 'low' (L) variety. He limits discussion of the problem, however, only to instances in which the 'high' variety also has 'a sizeable body of written literature' (330). In the event that this written literature in H is an older variety of L, the borrowing of lexemes from H into L is bound to show up as a seeming retardation in lexical replacement. Even here, however, I do not believe that writing is a NECESSARY condition for such a situation. A highly venerated oral literature which is passed from generation to generation by memorization provides an entirely comparable situation. Similarly a high form of speech used by privileged persons can exist side by side with a 'lower' form of speech spoken by common persons. For the Natchez Indians of Mississippi it has been reported that 'the speech of the Nobles differed from that of the lower orders'; John R. Swanton, *Indian tribes of the lower Mississippi Valley* ... 182 (= *Bureau of American Ethnology*, Bulletin 43) (Washington, 1911). Swanton's information is taken from Le Page du Pratz, *Histoire de la Louisiane*, 3 vols. (Paris, 1758) and he adds that "Du Pratz says 'this difference in language exists only in what concerns *the persons of the Suns and Nobles* in distinction from the people'". [Emphasis mine.] The decimation of the tribe at the hands of the French in the early eighteenth century brought on the breakdown of most of the old culture and it was impossible to confirm this in the 1930s when I worked with the last fluent speaker (now deceased). There are, however, a few ideas still expressed by two distinct terms and it is my guess that these may be all that is left of this example of preliterate diglossia in North America. Preliterate diglossia can also exist when the speech of men differs from that of women, since both sexes usually know both types of speech in order that male children can be taught by the mother as well as the father and that men as well as women can speak the proper forms when imitating female characters in telling myths; see, for example, my paper "Men's and women's speech in Koasati", *Lg.*, 20.142-9 (1944) (reprinted in *Language in culture and society*, ed. Dell Hymes 228-233, New York, Evanston and London, 1964).

have diverged in phonology, morphology, and lexicology in remarkably similar ways, then we can be sure that the lapse of time
needed to accomplish this has been comparable too. No, among
unwritten as well as written languages PREHISTORY IS WRITTEN IN
MILLENNIA, not decades.

We have already seen in section 1.6 that the Algonkian languages
(whose divergence is comparable to that of the Romance or
Germanic languages) have been written down since the early 1600's,
i.e. starting over three and a half centuries ago. If Pulgram's thesis
had a grain of truth, then Eliot's Natick Bible of 1663, now three
centuries old, would be written in a language far more archaic than
Proto-Algonkian itself; indeed it would be a kind of 'Hittite' of
Algonkian. Instead Natick is as close to Penobscot and other
nearby Algonkian languages as Swedish is to Danish, and Proto-
Algonkian cannot by any manner of means be reckoned as any less
ancient than Proto-Germanic. In innumerable instances where
American Indian linguists have checked words in early vocabularies
(100-300 or more years old) with the same words in languages still
spoken — Natick is no longer spoken — they have discovered no
appreciable change whatsoever. In other instances, minor sound
changes appear to have taken place, but in no instance are these
more drastic than those known to have taken place in European
(written) languages in a comparable period of time. One very
interesting example of such minor sound changes has been called
to my attention by my student, Allan Taylor, who collected a
vocabulary of Atsina[31] (a Plains Algonkian language varying only

---

[31] The Atsina forms quoted are taken from a comparative study of Arapaho
and Atsina presented by Allan R. Taylor at the Conference on Algonquian
Linguistics held at the National Museum of Canada, August 24-28, 1964. The
bracketed interpretation of the 1790 Atsina forms is my own. — The early forms
of Atsina are taken from Edward Umfreville, *The present state of the Hudson's
Bay*, 202 (London, 1790). The Proto-Algonkian forms are taken from Bloomfield's "Algonquian", 116-117 with the omission of the numeral suffix *-wi and
with the following changes in symbols: $P$ replaces $q$ and vowel length (e.g. $i$·)
replaces double vowels (e.g. $ii$). In many languages, e.g. Fox, Menomini,
Shawnee, Miami, Delaware, Powhatan, and Natick, the usual word for 'one'
is a descendant of PA *nekot-, but several other languages, e.g. Ojibwa, Abenaki,
Passamaquoddy, and Arapaho-Atsina, have words descended from PA *pe·šik-.

dialectically from Arapaho) and compared this with a vocabulary of the same language (same dialect) published nearly 200 years ago, in 1790 to be exact. The first four numerals are sufficient to illustrate the nature of these changes. Moreover, we also know the reconstructions of the Proto-Algonkian forms of these words and can thus compare both varieties of Atsina with these much older forms:

|        | Atsina (1960) | Atsina (1790)      | Proto-Algon. |
|--------|---------------|--------------------|--------------|
| one    | čέεθiy        | kar-ci [kɛɛsay]    | *pe·šik-     |
| two    | níiθ          | neece [niis]       | *ni·š-       |
| three  | nέεθ          | nar-ce [nɛɛs]      | *neʔθ-       |
| four   | yέεn          | ne-an [ni(y)ɛɛn]   | *nye·w-      |

Early Atsina $k$ > modern $č$ (before front vowels), early Ats. $s$ > modern $θ$, and the initial syllable of 'four' has dropped. But the changes that have taken place between PA and early Atsina are far more drastic: PA *$p$ > early Ats. $k$ everywhere (modern $k$ before back vowels, $č$ before front vowels); PA *$š$ > early Ats. $s$ (> $θ$); PA *$-ʔθ-$ > early Ats. $s$ (> $θ$); PA *$w$ > $n$ (in 'four' and many other words).

# 2. PROTOLANGUAGES AND PROBLEMS OF RECONSTRUCTION

## 2.1 WHAT IS A PROTOLANGUAGE?

The answer, quite simply, is that any language is an actual or potential protolanguage. Two or three thousand years hence — barring catastrophic changes — a variety of languages stemming from English will be spoken in wide areas of the globe, areas more or less delineating those in which English is now spoken as a first language. The same can be said, with appropriate modifications in regard to size of area, of Spanish, Portuguese, Russian, and Chinese, not to speak of Hindi, Tamil, Kikuyu, and a host of others.

Given the lapse of a sufficient amount of time, this means (1) that the descendants of these languages, if still spoken, will have diverged enough to be compared and used in the reconstruction of their respective parent languages, and (2) that the result of such reconstruction will provide a body of material that is recognizably like the English, Spanish, Portuguese, etc. spoken today. It will not, however, be identical with what appears in written records. Linguistic change takes place in the SPOKEN language and the written language always lags far behind in recording this change, in large part, of course, to retain the tremendous advantages of the fiction of cohesiveness in the linguistic community as long as possible, in spite of ever-increasing differences in the spoken language. The word 'mayor' is spelled m-a-y-o-r from London to Vancouver and from Atlanta to Brisbane, even though the actual pronunciation of the word may vary so widely as to be unrecognizable out of context (or possibly even in context) if persons of different areas chance to meet. Furthermore, dozens of words and turns of expression having only local provenience may never chance to be recorded anywhere but will persist in their own areas completely uninfluenced by the fact that they did not find a place in the written language of today. Still more important, there are many things which will inevitably be lost in all the daughter languages and thus be unrecoverable by the comparative method. These are the reasons why Proto-Romance is not in all details identical with recorded Latin. But this fact, far from being an indictment of the comparative method is an elegant example of its tremendous power.

Every protolanguage was in the same way once a real language, whether or not we are fortunate enough to have written records of it. Furthermore, even when we do have written records, we find that what we are able to reconstruct of a given protolanguage always falls short of giving us the full picture of the real language it stands for. But written records fall short, too, as we have seen in the case of local pronunciation variations, lexical items, and turns of expression, and reconstruction methods can and do, in fact, give us information about parent languages not to be found in written records. We are of course twice blessed when we have both, as in the case of Proto-Romance and Latin. When we have only the reconstructed protolanguage, however, we still have a glorious artifact, one which is far more precious than anything an archeologist can ever hope to unearth.

A protolanguage, then, is reconstructed out of the evidence that is acquired by the careful comparison of the daughter languages and, in the beginning of the work, what is reconstructed reflects what can be discovered by working backwards in those cases where all or most of the daughter languages point to the same conclusion. This provides the initial framework. Once this is established, the principle of analogy can be drawn upon, and by its use instances in which there are aberrations, statistically speaking, can often also be plausibly accounted for. Deductive as well as inductive hypotheses must be constructed and checked. Then when all the comparisons that can reasonably be made have been made, and when all the reconstructions that can reasonably be made have been made, the result is a PROTOTYPICAL MODEL OF THE DAUGHTER LANGUAGES, or, what we normally call a protolanguage.

If we turn the whole thing round and look at it from the other direction we see that the daughter languages are not only different from each other but also from the protolanguage. We describe this differentiation by calling it 'linguistic change'. In phonology, linguistic change normally shows such regularity that it is possible to formulate what the nineteenth century linguists proudly called 'phonetic laws' on the analogy of what their fellow natural scientists were with equal pride referring to as 'laws of nature',[1] even though, as Sapir once remarked, "... phonetic laws are by no means comparable to the laws of physics or chemistry or any other of the natural sciences. They are merely general statements of a series of changes characteristic of a given language at a particular time."[2] The most impressive characteristic of phonetic laws, or statements of phonetic correspondences, is their power to predict[3] — not the future of a language, to be sure, but the phonetic shape of a cognate in any language for which the correspondences are known. Other types of linguistic change do not operate with the same kind of predictable regularity; perhaps it would be better to say that we have not yet arrived at the point of being able to make statements about other types of linguistic change in such a way as to reveal such a power. Change can occur in inflection and in other parts of morphology. It can occur in meaning and in vocabulary. But since it has not yet become possible to make predictable statements about any of these kinds of changes, the verifiable regularity of sound correspondences is seen to be even more precious than it may have seemed at first.

[1] Present-day scientific philosophers are also quick to point out the imprecision, though not necessarily the uselessness, of the term 'law of nature'. Thus Ernest Nagel, in *The structure of science* (New York-Burlingame, 1960), says: "The label 'law of nature' (or similar labels such as 'scientific law', 'natural law', or simply 'law') *is not a technical term defined in any empirical science...*". (49) [Emphasis mine.]
[2] "The concept of phonetic law ...", 73 (of reprint).
[3] Sapir stresses this in "The concept of phonetic law ..." when he says that Bloomfield's "setting-up of phonetic law No. 6 was, by implication, *a theoretically possible prediction* of a distinct and discoverable phonetic pattern. The prediction was based essentially on the assumption of the regularity of sound change in language", 78 (of reprint). [Emphasis mine.]

In the sections which follow problems of both phonological and morphological reconstruction are discussed, with examples taken largely from the Muskogean and Algonkian families of languages.

## 2.2 SOUND CHANGE

### 2.21 The Muskogean family of languages

This family[4] formerly flourished in the southeastern part of what is now the United States. There are four distinct languages still

TABLE I

*Combined chart of the consonants and vowels of four Muskogean languages*

|  | Bilabial | Dental | Alveolar | Palatal | Velar | Faucal |
|---|---|---|---|---|---|---|
| Voiceless | p  p | t  t |  | č  c | k  k |  |
| Stops | p  p | t  t |  | c  c | k  k |  |
| Voiced | b  b |  |  |  |  |  |
| Stops | b  — |  |  |  |  |  |
| Voiceless | f  f | ł  ł | s  — | š  s |  | h  h |
| Spirants | f  f | ł  ł | —  — | s  s |  | h  h |
| Voiced Nasal | m  m | n  n |  |  |  |  |
| Continuants | m  m | n  n |  |  | -ŋ  -ŋ |  |
| Voiced Nonnasal | w  w | l  l |  | y  y |  | .  . |
| Continuants | w  w | l  l |  | y  y |  | .  . |
| Vowels | u  u |  |  | i  i |  | a  a |
|  | u  u |  |  | i  i |  | a  a |

[4] See Mary R. Haas, "The classification of the Muskogean languages", *Language, culture, and personality*, eds. Leslie Spier, A. Irving Hallowell, and Stanley S. Newman, 41-56 (Menasha, Wisconsin, 1941). The paper sets forth most of the sound correspondences with examples, but full reconstructions are seldom given. Other extant 'languages' of the Muskogean family are but dialect variants of these, viz. Chickasaw (almost identical with Choctaw, but spoken by a separate political body), Alabama (very close to Koasati but spoken by a separate political body), Mikasuki (very close to Hitchiti but spoken by a separate group), and Seminole (almost identical with Creek but spoken by the descendants of those who fled to the Everglades during the Indian wars).

extant, so by accident we have a neat workable set of languages without being constrained to choose among them. They are Choctaw (Ch), Koasati (K), Hitchiti (H), and Creek (C). As an aid to the understanding of the illustrative sound changes, Table I shows the combined consonant and vowel charts[5] of the four languages arranged in quadrant form (in each box) for convenience, viz.

$$\frac{\text{Ch} \mid \text{K}}{\text{H} \mid \text{C}}$$

In Table II[6] several sets of items having the same gloss are taken from these four Muskogean languages and the illustrations used in the sections which follow are based on this material.

TABLE II

*Sample sets of cognates in four Muskogean languages*

|  | 1. sun | 2. sleep | 3. arrow | 4. night | 5. day | 6. mulberry |
|---|---|---|---|---|---|---|
| Ch | haši | nusi | naki | ninak | nittak | bihi |
| K | hasi | nuci | łaki | niła(hasi)'moon' | nihta | bihi(cuba) 'fig' |
| H | ha·s(i) | nu·c(í·ki) | (in)łak(i) | ni·łak(i) | nihtak(i) | bi[h]- (Sn) |
| C | hási | nuc(ita) | łí· | niłí· | nittá· | kí· |
| PM | *hasi | *nuci | *Naki | *niNaki | *nihtaka | *kʷihi |

[5]   A dash is used in Table I when a given language lacks a certain sound. Choctaw is the only one of the four languages which distinguishes an alveolar and a palatal sibilant. The other languages have a single sibilant which may range from alveolar to palatal but is frequently more palatal and is therefore placed in that column. Vowel length, symbolized by a raised dot (·), configurates like a voiced nonnasal continuant in all the languages and for that reason is placed in that row on the chart.

[6]   The following conventions are used in Table II. A linguistic item placed in parentheses is a separate morph, not entering into the comparison, which often or usually co-occurs with the morph being compared. In Koasati *nila-* is not the usual word for 'night' but occurs only in certain special combinations, e.g. with *hasi* 'sun' in the word quoted; *cuba* 'big' is combined with *bihi-*, not recorded separately, in the quoted word for 'fig'. In Hitchiti *-i* is a suffix used with all nouns; *-i·ki* is the infinitive marker for verbs; *in-* in the quoted word for 'arrow' is the third person possessive marker in alienable possession; and *-an* in 'two' is a numeral suffix. In Creek *-ita* is the infinitive marker for verbs. An item placed in square brackets is inferred or 'reconstituted'; thus *bi[h]-* occurs only in *bi hasi* 'mulberry month', taken from ms. materials of John R. Swanton (Sn), and it is assumed that the single *h* actually should be two: *bi[h]hasi.*

|  | 7. fish | 8. squirrel | 9. two | 10. go through | 11. snake | 12. wide |
|---|---|---|---|---|---|---|
| Ch | nani | fani | tuklu | łupul(li) | sinti | patha |
| K | łału | ipłu | tuklu | łuput(li) | cintu | patha |
| H | la·ł(i) | hï·ł(i) | tukl(an) | —— | cint(i) | —— |
| C | łáłu | íłu | hukkul(íta) | łupu·t(t-) | cíttu | táph(i·) |
| PM | *NaNi/u | *ixʷaNi/u | *hutukulu | *łupu(·)t- | *cinti/u | *patha |

|  | 13. pumpkin | 14. boat | 15. duck | 16. male | 17. land |
|---|---|---|---|---|---|
| Ch | šukši | pi·ni | fucuš | nakni | yakni |
| K | cuksi | piłła | cus(kani) | na·ni | iha·ni |
| H | cuks(i) | pił(i) | fu·c(i) | nakn(i) | yakn(i) |
| C | cási | piłłu | fúcu | (hu)nánwa | i·kaná |
| PM | *cuksi | *pinNi/a/u | *xʷučus | *nakniwa | *ihakanika |

## 2.22 Paradigmatic vs. syntagmatic sound change

Sound change is often characterized as being of two types, (1) regular and (2) sporadic, and the first is sometimes further described as 'gradual' and the second as 'sudden'. Since the second type is usually said to include such phenomena as assimilation and dissimilation as well as metathesis, epenthesis, syncope, and the like, it is clear that the regular vs. sporadic dichotomy cannot be fitted exactly with the gradual vs. sudden one, for some types of assimilation may very well take place gradually while metathesis, epenthesis, syncope, and the like, cannot occur in any fashion other than suddenly.[7]

---

[7] It is a curious thing that many linguists take the view that there is something basically unacceptable about sudden sound change. It is therefore refreshing to find that Paul Kiparsky, in his recent paper on "Sonorant clusters in Greek", *Lg.*, 43.619-35 (1967), takes a different tack: "I cannot see that metathesis is in any way an 'unrealistic' form of sound change ... . If metatheses are to be excluded on general grounds, one wonders what intermediate stage would have to be postulated for *tíktō* < *títkō* 'beget', and even more so in cases where the metathesis is between non-contiguous segments, e.g. *sképtomai* < *spek-* 'look at'. In any case the only general grounds on which I can conceive anybody wanting to exclude metatheses would be the position that sound change is necessarily a gradual process, a position which is falsified at least by the existence of epenthesis, syncope, etc. as forms of sound change." (pp. 622-23, footnote 3).

It seems to me that it might be more revealing to show phonological change on two axes, the SYNTAGMATIC (horizontal) and the PARADIGMATIC (vertical). According to this model, assimilation, dissimilation, metathesis, prothesis, epenthesis, and the like (see 2.3), are arranged on the syntagmatic axis while so-called vowel and consonant 'shifts' or correspondences are placed on the paradigmatic axis.

Illustrations of Muskogean sound correspondences, i.e. the paradigmatic axis, are taken up first. The items for 'fish', no. 7 (Table II), comprise a perfect set of cognates. The sound correspondences are as follows:

(1) Ch $n$ : K, H, C $l$. See also 'arrow', no. 3; 'night', no. 4 (second cons.); and 'squirrel', no. 8. The symbol $*N$ has been chosen as the reconstruction for the $n$ : $l$ correspondence. The symbol $*n$ is needed when all the languages show $n$, e.g. 'sleep', no. 2; 'night', no. 4 (first cons.). Similarly, $*l$ is needed when all have $l$, e.g. 'go through', no. 10.

(2) Ch, K, and C short vowel in initial open syllable : H long vowel. See also 'sun', no. 1; 'sleep', no. 2; and 'night', no. 4. This is reconstructed as a short vowel.

(3) Ch final $i$ : K, H, C final $u$. See also 'squirrel', no. 8; 'snake', no. 11. This correspondence is found only in final syllables and is symbolized in reconstruction as $*i/u$. Some final syllables show $i$ in all languages and for these $*i$ is reconstructed; see 'sun', no. 1. Similarly for $*u$; see, in part, 'two', no. 9, where Ch and K both have $u$.

In terms of these correspondences and the symbols chosen to represent them, the full PM reconstruction for 'fish' is $*NaNi/u$.

Other sets of cognates shown in Table II illustrate still other regularities in correspondences.

The usual correspondences for Choctaw $s$, $š$ and the affricate $c$ [č] are as follows:

(4) Ch $š$:K, H, C $s$; see 'sun', no. 1; 'pumpkin', no. 13; 'duck', no. 15. PM $*s$.

(5) Ch $s$:K, H, C $c$ (affricate); see 'sleep', no. 2; 'snake', no. 11. 'Pumpkin', no. 13, shows Ch $š$ instead of $s$ but this is the result of assimilation to the $š$ of the following syllable. PM *$c$.

(6) Ch $c$:K, H, C $c$; see 'duck', no. 15. PM *$č$.

A different alignment occurs for Choctaw $b$ (see 2.421):

(7) Ch, K, H $b$:C $k$; see 'mulberry', no. 6. PM *$k^w$ (PM *$x^w$, as in 'duck', no. 15, is set up instead of *$f$ to pattern with *$k^w$.)

### 2.23 *The syntagmatic axis*

Turning now to the sound changes that are best shown on the syntagmatic axis, we can illustrate assimilation, dissimilation and metathesis. Assimilation is shown horizontally by the use of a straight arrow; it is directed to the right (→) for assimilation to what follows and to the left (←) for assimilation to what precedes. Dissimilation is shown by a bar; it is placed on the right ( ⊣ ) or on the left ( ⊢ ) in accordance with the same principle. Finally, metathesis is shown by a looped arrow, to the right (↻) or to the left (↺). In Table II examples of consonantic assimilation resulting in gemination are seen in 'day' (both Ch and C), no. 5; 'two' (C), no. 9 (see also Table IIIb); and 'snake' (C), no. 11. Thus for 'snake' we have:

PM *$cinti/u$ : pre-C *$cin{\rightarrow}tu$ : C *$cíttu$.

Dissimilation is rare. An example is seen in 'squirrel' (K), no. 8, more fully discussed in 2.24:

PM *$ix^waNi/u$ : pre-K *$if{\dashv}lu$ : K $iplu$.

Metathesis, on the other hand, is fairly common, particularly between subdialects of Choctaw and Creek. In Table II there is one example, viz. 'wide' (C), no. 12:

PM *$patha$ : pre-C *$p{\circlearrowright}a\ th(i\cdot)$ : C $táph(i\cdot)$

## 2.3 PHONOLOGICAL LOSS AND ADDITION

### 2.31 *Types of loss and addition*

Sometimes it is necessary to employ considerable ingenuity to obtain the reconstruction which will account for ALL the differences among the daughter languages. In addition to different articulatory features associated with the various vowels and consonants, as when *n* corresponds to *l*, it is often necessary to reckon with other kinds of phonological change. For example, even though the stems of all the daughter languages show two syllables for a certain item it may turn out that the prototype language had three (or even more) syllables.

This situation may result from contraction (2.32) or from other kinds of attrition, including syncope (2.33), apocope (2.34), and apheresis (2.35). On the other hand, the protolanguage may have fewer syllables than one or more of the daughter languages as the result of prothesis and epenthesis (2.36).

### 2.32 *Contraction*

As a case in point, let us look at the word for 'night', no. 4 in Table II. Although no problem is encountered in comparing $V_1$ in all four languages, a first glance at $V_2$ seems to show a special correspondence, viz. Ch, K, H *a* : C *i·*. But a look at the word for 'day', no. 5, reveals that there is also a correspondence of Ch, K, H *a* : C *a·*. An examination of the environment in which both correspondences appear (i.e. stem final position) enables us to make a somewhat improved statement that Ch, H *ak*, K *a* : C *i·* or *a·*. The proper solution, however, does not become clear until we study the word for 'arrow', no. 3, a disyllable. Here the correspondence is:

Ch, K *aki*, H *ak* : C *i·*

and we see that when Creek has *i·* the prototype must have been *\*aki*, as in Choctaw. Choctaw and Koasati final *i* appear for prototype final *\*i* in disyllabic words only; in words of more than two syllables, Choctaw lacks final *i* and Koasati lacks not only final *i* but the preceding *k* as well. Using the disyllabic word 'arrow', no. 3, as a model we can then assume that the prototype for 'night', no. 4, also ended in *aki* even though in this instance Creek provides our only clue to the identity of the final vowel.[8] This leads to the proper reconstruction of the word for 'night' as a trisyllabic *ni-Naki*, even though all the daughter languages have reduced it to a disyllabic word.

A similar solution can be worked out for the word for 'day', no. 5. In this instance no disyllabic word has been found as an aid in the solution, but we do not need it. If Creek *i·* is the contraction of *aki* in 'night', then Creek *a·* must be the contraction of *aka* in 'day'. We can then confidently reconstruct the prototype for 'day' as *nihtaka*.

For those who still insist that they would like to see more tangible evidence to support such a reconstruction, it turns out that this can be supplied precisely for the word for 'day'. When Europeans first arrived in North America, the Muskogean family appears to have comprised more languages than have been preserved in spoken form down to the present day. How many more is not known. One such extinct language is Apalachee. It is known to us through a bilingual letter (Spanish and Apalachee) bearing the date January 21, 1688 which was written for transmittal to King Charles II. On the basis of this letter it is possible to determine not only that Apalachee was Muskogean but also that it was closest to Alabama-Koasati. The word for 'day', as written by a Spanish-speaking scribe nearly three centuries ago was n-i-h-t-a-g-a, a clear confirmation of the reconstructed *nihtaka*.

## 2.33 *Syncope*

A more complex problem is posed by the word for 'squirrel', no. 8. If we had only Choctaw *fani* and Creek *ihu* we might be tempted to dismiss the forms as noncognate except for the nagging fact that

---

[8]    Mary R. Haas, "The historical development of certain long vowels in Creek", *IJAL*, 16.122-5 (1950). This solution had not yet become clear to me at the time "The classification..." was written.

Ch $n$ : C $l$ and Ch final $i$ : C final $u$ are both well-attested correspondences. Even so it would probably be very difficult to make a satisfactory full reconstruction without the neat evidence supplied by Koasati *iplu*. This allows us to make a hypothesis about the sound correspondences among the three which can best be shown in a vertical arrangement, as in the lefthand column of Table IIIa. Again we seem to have a trisyllabic word as the prototype even though all the daughter languages have a disyllabic word, but the

TABLE IIIa

*Proto-Muskogean 'squirrel'*

| Ch | f | a | n | i | | | | | *ø | xʷ | a | N | i/u |
|---|---|---|---|---|---|---|---|---|---|---|---|---|---|
| K | i | p | ł | u | *i | f | | ł | u | *i | xʷ | ø | N | i/u |
| H | h | ï· | | ł- | *i | ø | | ł- | | *i | xʷ | ø | N | i/u |
| C | í | | | ł | u | *i | ø | | ł | u | *i | xʷ | ø | N | i/u |
| | | | | | | | | | | | | | | |
| PM | *i | xʷ | a | N | i/u | | | | | *i | xʷ | a | N | i/u |

reduction rules needed are quite different from those for 'night', no. 4, and 'day', no. 5. Choctaw has lost the vowel of the first syllable (symbolized by ø in the righthand column) and Koasati, Hitchiti and Creek have lost that of the second syllable. The loss of the second vowel leaves a cluster of two spirants, $f$ and $l$ (as shown in the middle column). Koasati shows dissimilation in manner of articulation and replaces $f$ with the homorganic stop $p$; Hitchiti and Creek have dropped it.[9] The prototype word for 'squirrel' is *$ix^waNi/u$.

Solving the problem of the reconstruction of the word for 'squirrel' turns out to provide a clue to the problem of the reconstruction of the word for 'two'. If Choctaw has lost the FIRST vowel and Koasati, Hitchiti, and Creek the SECOND vowel in the trisyllabic prototype for 'squirrel', is it possible that longer words might show the loss of odd-numbered vowels in some languages as against the loss of even-numbered vowels in others? In other words, allowing

---

[9]  Hitchiti *hï·l(i)* has the usual lengthened vowel for a prototype initial open syllable, but the nasalization is unexplained. The initial $h$ is common in this language as the onset before a vowel. The Hitchiti form has thus lost as much of the prototype material as has Creek.

for the fact that final vowels are not subject to syncope, is the vocalic syncope in 'squirrel' actually an instance of ALTERNATIVE SYNCOPE? If we show the probable sound correspondences among the words for 'two' in a vertical fashion, we have the arrangement shown in the lefthand column of Table IIIb. Choctaw, Koasati, and Hitchiti have syncopated the first and third vowels, Creek the second, as is shown by ø in the righthand column of the table. Pre-Creek had a two-stop cluster *tk, as shown in the middle column, and *t has assimilated to *k in position of articulation giving the geminate cluster kk in modern Creek. The reconstruction which most adequately accounts for all the modern attested forms for 'two' is *hutukulu.

TABLE IIIb
*Proto-Muskogean 'two'*

| Ch, K | t u k   l u | | *ø t u k ø l u |
|---|---|---|---|
| H | t u k   l- | | *ø t u k ø l- |
| C | h u k   k u l- | *h u t → k u l- | *h u t ø k u l- |
| PM | *h u t u k u l u | | *h u t u k u l u |

2.34 *Apocope*

Loss of vowels in word-final position is a characteristic of several Algonkian languages, but some of them show an even greater amount of attrition due to the regressive unvoicing of finals in which consonants and consonant clusters as well as vowels are lost. As soon as a final consonant or consonant cluster is lost, there is a new final vowel which is in its turn unvoiced and subject to loss. So ..VCVCV → ..VCVC → ..VCV → ..VC, e.g. F aškote·wi, C iskote·w, O iškote·, Ps skwət 'fire', and ..VCCVCV → ..VCCVC → ..VCCV → ..VC(C), e.g. F ahkani, C oskan, Ch heko, A hix 'bone'; see 'fire' and 'bone' in Table IV.[10]

[10] Abbreviations for the names of languages used in Table IV are as follows: A, Arapaho; C, Cree; Ch, Cheyenne; D, Delaware; F, Fox; K, Kickapoo; M, Menomini; Mi, Miami; O, Ojibwa; Pn, Penobscot; Ps, Passamaquoddy; PA, Proto-Algonkian. The sound correspondences illustrated in the table are regular and those for Fox, Cree, Menomini, and Ojibwa are fully discussed in

TABLE IV.

The Algonkian words for 'fire', 'bone', 'water', and 'snow'

| | fire | bone | water | snow |
|---|---|---|---|---|
| PA | *e š k o t e· w i<br>*e š kwete· w i | *o θ k a n i<br>*wa θ k a n i | *n e p y i | *k o· n y a |
| Mi | k o t ä w i | a k a n i | | |
| F | a š k o t e· w i | a h k a n i | n e p i | |
| K | o s k o t e· w i | o h k a n i | | ok o· n a |
| C | i s k o t e· w | o s k a n | n i piy | k o· n a |
| M | e s k o t ɛ· w | o h k a· n | n e pe·w | k o· n(y) |
| O | i š k o t e· | o k k a n | n imp i | ak o· n |
| Ch | ho ʔ e t a | he k o | m ahp e | |
| A | (hi)s í t ee | hi x | n é č | hí ií |
| D | | x k a n | m p í | k u· n |
| Pn | s kwɔt e | | n ɔ p i | |
| Ps | s kwɔt | s k ɔ n | | |

2.35 *Apheresis*

The loss of a short initial vowel (apheresis) is illustrated in several of the Algonkian words for 'fire' in the same table, viz. Miami, Penobscot, Passamoquoddy, and one of the Arapaho alternants. The Muskogean languages show not only initial vowel loss but initial syllable loss; see 'duck', no. 15 in Table II, which exemplifies such loss in Koasati.

2.36 *Prothesis and epenthesis*

The addition of an initial (prothetic) vowel, consonant, or syllable is also exemplified in the Algonkian languages. Consonant addition is seen in Cheyenne and Arapaho where

PA #V → hV

in all instances; see 'fire' and 'bone' in Table IV. The same rule applies to Hitchiti among the Muskogean languages; see Table IIIa.

Bloomfield's "Algonquian" (1946). Those needing special note are: PA *k → A Ø; both *o and *i → A i; PA *e, *a, *o (and *i) → Ch a, o, e, respectively. See also my paper, "Vowels and semivowels in Algonkian", *Lg.*, 42.479-488 (1966).

Kickapoo, Ojibwa, and Arapaho add a prothetic vowel in 'snow' in Table IV, but the conditions under which this takes place are unknown.

The addition of a vowel or consonant in the middle of a word is known as epenthesis. Cree has epenthetic *i* according to regular rule

PA ..Cy → ..Ciy

and Menomini appears to have a similar rule except that it is limited to the second syllable:

PA (CV)Cy → pre-M (CV)Ciy → (CV)Cew(h)

See the Cree and Menomini words for 'water' in Table IV. The lengthening of the vowel of the second syllable is the result of a separate rule which does not concern us here.

Epenthetic homorganic nasals seem to be a regular development in Ojibwa, so that (letting N = nasal, S = stop or spirant) we have

PA NVS → NVN→S.

Cheyenne developed in a similar way but requires a further rule stating that

Pre-Ch NVN→S → N→VN→S → NVhS

In other words, in pre-Cheyenne the first nasal assimilated to the homorganic epenthetic nasal and then the second nasal was replaced by *h*. See 'water' in Table IV.

## 2.4 RECONSTRUCTION AND REALITY

### 2.41 *Approximating a real language*

The examples from Muskogean and Algonkian given in the preceding section illustrate the same regularity of phonological change that has now become familiar in Indo-European, Uto-Aztecan, and many other language families. They also serve to illustrate two important differences between a REAL language and a reconstructed protolanguage.

(1) If I could hear Proto-Muskogean spoken I would know the precise phonetic quality of the consonant I can now only

symbolize as *$N$, or in full as Ch $n$ : K, H, C $l$. This lack of precision, however, is trivial because there can be no doubt that there was a distinctive protoconsonant characterized by some feature of $n$ and some feature of $l$. The symbol used reflects this.

(2) If I could hear Proto-Muskogean spoken I would also know the precise nature of the final syllable or syllables of the words for 'fish', no. 7, and 'squirrel', no. 8 (in Table II) which can now be symbolized only awkwardly as *$i/u$. But with more evidence from some direction I could make a change in the reconstruction in a nontrivial fashion, e.g. by adding something to it.

A reconstructed protolanguage is an approximation to a real language but it always falls short of being identical with the actual prototype language. The phones of a real language and the morphs of a real language ARE as they have been recorded at a given moment of time, whether that moment was the record made by a trained fieldworker yesterday or by a scribe in ancient times. The reconstructed phones and the reconstructed morphs of a proto-language are of course expected to represent the best efforts of scholars in approximating the reality of these entities. But more evidence, or different evidence — the discovery of a new daughter language, for instance — can bring new insights which may at any time make it necessary to change the reconstruction of a phone or of a morph. And when this happens the reconstruction MUST be changed. In this way the approximation to the reality can be increased even if never reached. What can be reconstructed of a protolanguage is thus comparable to the visible part of an iceberg; only a greater or lesser percentage is recoverable in spite of the certainty that the reality was both quantitatively and qualitatively much richer. In this respect historical linguistics is like archeology. In the one case it is impossible to recover the living flesh of the spoken language that was the prototype, in the other it is impossible to reify the processes of social interaction that belonged to the particular horizon.

## 2.42  *Need to change reconstructions*

It was mentioned above that reconstructions can be changed on the basis of new insights. But where are these new insights to come from? Some of the most likely possibilities are discussed in the following paragraphs.

2.421    (1) *A new interpretation of the material on hand.* — A new hypothesis about the interpretation of some recalcitrant facets of the material already available can be developed. The most celebrated example of this is Saussure's postulation in 1879 of a schwa (ə) to help regularize the statements about the development of certain Indo-European vowels. It was nearly fifty years later that Kuryłowicz[11] proposed to identify this with the transcribed *h* of Hittite, on which materials, unknown to Saussure of course, had only recently been discovered.

A less spectacular example can be taken from Table II in connection with the Muskogean word for 'mulberry', no. 6. Because of a very limited number of examples (many of which had other problems) the cognation of Choctaw *bihi* and Creek *kí·* was not immediately recognized. But the postulation of a PM labiovelar consonant $*k^w$ (> Ch, K, and H *b*, C *k*) provided an entirely satisfactory solution to the problem.[12] A glance at Table I shows that *b*, as the only voiced stop, skews the configuration of stops in Choctaw, Koasati, and Hitchiti. But the postulation of $*k^w$ for PM completely eliminates the necessity of retaining that skewing in the protolanguage:

[11]  Jerzy Kuryłowicz, "ə Indoeuropéen et *h* Hittite", *Symbolae grammaticae offertes à J. Rozwadowski*, 95-104 (1927).

[12]  The most unusual thing about this sound correspondence is that it splits the Muskogean family along lines which differ from the split attested in a number of other sound correspondences. The deepest split is apparently between Choctaw-Chickasaw as the Western division, on the one hand, and Alabama-Koasati, Hitchiti-Mikasuki, and Creek-Seminole as the Eastern division, on the other hand. This is illustrated in nos. 1, 2, 3, 4, 7, 8, and 14 in Table II and is discussed in more detail in "The classification ...", 43-5. The *b*: *k* correspondence, however, keeps Alabama-Koasati, and Hitchiti-Mikasuki with Choctaw-Chickasaw and separates Creek-Seminole from all the rest. See also Mary R. Haas, "Development of Proto-Muskogean $*k^w$", *IJAL*, 13.135-7 (1947).

PM voiceless stops and affricates: $*p *t *c *\check{c} *k *k^w$

In this case we can never hope to recover documentary evidence to confirm the hypothesis, though we may some day be fortunate enough to find support through extrafamilial comparison; see 2.423 below.

2.422  (2) *The discovery of a new daughter language.* — The discovery of a new daughter language signals the need to reexamine all previous work in the light of the new evidence. Unbelievable as it may seem, this is all too seldom done. If the body of reconstructed material already in existence is extensive, the attempt will be made to fit the new language into the already established scheme in so far as it is possible to do so. There will be a strong temptation to explain away the things that do not fit the old scheme as aberrations of the newly discovered language. It is of course always possible that they are, but this should never be taken for granted. The new language must be studied not only in relation to the reconstructed material but also in relation to all of the previously known daughter languages. If this is done, it may very well turn out that some reconstructions will be seen to be faulty or some phases of the morphology of the protolanguage will be defective or biased in the direction of certain daughter languages. In all such circumstances changes in the reconstructed scheme will have to be made. To put it in other words, instead of trimming the new material to fit the old scheme, one must modify the old scheme to accommodate the new material. Even in Indo-European, the best studied family of them all, scholars are lagging far behind in their exploitation of the important new material that has become available to them in the twentieth century. Tocharian, for example, "has contributed little to our knowledge of Indo-European", according to Lehmann, because "most of the basic research ... has been undertaken only recently".[13] But until Tocharian, and Hittite, and all the other unexploited Indo-European language materials, have been exhaustively studied for all the information they can yield, we are obliged to confess that our knowledge of Proto-Indo-

[13]  Lehmann, *Historical linguistics*, 38.

European is far less adequate than it would need to be. Indeed this lag in the articulation of newly discovered materials (often chronologically older) with the more thoroughly worked materials (often chronologically younger) explains the persistent uncertainty about the meaning of the aberrancies of Hittite which have ranged from the hypothesis that Hittite was a sister language of Indo-European (the so-called 'Indo-Hittite hypothesis')[14] to "speculation that Hittite may be a Creole, i.e., the descendant of a Pidgin originally used for communication between speakers of Indo-European and non-Indo-European languages in Anatolia".[15]

2.423   (3) *Evidence from old loanwords.* — In the historical study of written languages it is commonplace to make use of evidence from loanwords, outloans as well as inloans. This potentially valuable source of information has been almost totally neglected in the study of unwritten languages,[16] not because such information is not available but because the drudgery of patient sifting of many sources has all too often been neglected.[17]

In his reconstruction of Proto-Algonkian Bloomfield set up a large number of medial consonant clusters. The first member of many of these is represented by an arbitrary symbol (e.g. $x$ in *$xk$, *$xp$) or by a symbol not to be identified with its independent mate (e.g. $\theta$ in *$\theta k$ which is not to be identified with prevocalic *$\theta$). It is clear that one of the most urgent problems of internal reconstruc-

---

[14]   Edgar H. Sturtevant, *The Indo-Hittite laryngeals*, 23-8 (Baltimore, 1942); "The pronoun *$so$, *$sā$, *$tod$ and the Indo-Hittite hypothesis", *Lg.*, 15.11-9 (1939), and other writings. Sturtevant credits Emil Forrer with having first advanced the hypothesis in 1921.
[15]   Warren Cowgill, "Universals in Indo-European diachronic morphology", *Universals of Language*, ed. Joseph H. Greenberg, 91-113 (Cambridge, 1963). The quotation is on p. 101.
[16]   This applies when both the donor language and the recipient language is unwritten. Loans from written languages like Sanskrit have frequently been traced in unwritten as well as written languages of India and Southeast Asia.
[17]   Frank T. Siebert has recently presented some material on Algonkian-Siouan borrowing in "Discrepant Consonant Clusters Ending in *-$k$ in Proto-Algonquian", pp. 48-59, in *Contributions to Anthropology: Linguistics*, 1 (= *National Museum of Canada, Bulletin* 214, 1967).

tion within Proto-Algonkian is the proper identification of these arbitrary symbols with actual phonemes.

Bloomfield has shown that within Proto-Algonkian, $*t$ - $k$ → $*\theta k$.[18] This leads us to think that a more realistic reconstruction of $*\theta k$ might be $*tk$. Perhaps there is also outside evidence for this in the Natchez word ?emet 'beaver' which is possibly the descendant of an old loan from PA $*ame\theta kwa$ 'beaver'; better $*ametkwa$ (?). (Natchez has widespread harmonization of vowels within stems and this accounts for the identity of the vowels in the Natchez word.)

2.424   (4) *The comparison of one protolanguage with another.* — The most challenging way in which new insight into reconstruction can be achieved comes about when one protolanguage is compared with another protolanguage, or, as often happens, when a proto-language is compared with a single language lacking near relatives.[19] This type of comparison can truly be said to be one of the most important new frontiers of historical and comparative linguistics.

Even in the nineteenth century, Indo-Europeanists were already aware that this was likely to be the next step — witness the suggestions of a genetic relationship between Indo-European and Hamito-Semitic, or between Indo-European and Finno-Ugric — but Indo-Europeanists have not really led the way in this field. An important early piece of work was the Whorf-Trager comparison of reconstructed Uto-Aztecan forms with reconstructed Tanoan forms.[20] More recently it is probable that more has been done in comparing some of the protolanguages of Mexico than those anywhere else.[21]

---

[18]  "Algonquian", p. 91.

[19]  In other words, an isolated language or a 'language isolate' (see 3.12).

[20]  B. L. Whorf and G. L. Trager, "The relationship of Uto-Aztecan and Tanoan", *American Anthropologist*, 39.609-24 (1937). They describe what they have done in the following terms: "But by reconstructing the ancestral forms of each family, and then by comparative methods delving still deeper into the past, we discover the common ancestor of both. The fundamental matrix of relationships is exposed, and it becomes possible for scholars to proceed on finer and finer lines in order to make historical deductions and reveal time time perspectives" (610).

[21]  See, for example, Robert E. Longacre, "Amplification of Gudschinsky's Proto-Popolocan-Mixtecan", *IJAL*, 28.227-42 (1962) and the references to

When two or more protolanguages are compared (or when one or more protolanguages and one or more 'language isolates' are compared) they are treated like daughter languages of a still earlier protolanguage. In other words, the investigator is seeking to establish an earlier 'common horizon'.[22] Little work of this kind has been done among families north of Mexico since the afore-mentioned effort of Whorf and Trager. However, a small beginning has been made in the comparison of Proto-Algonkian and Proto-Muskogean,[23] and Table V shows a comparison of a certain

TABLE V

'Fish', 'squirrel', and 'tree' in Proto-Algonkian and Proto-Muskogean

|  | fish | squirrel | tree |
|---|---|---|---|
| PA | *n a m e· k w- | *a n i k w- | *m e ʔ t e k w- |
| PM | *N a N i / u | *i xʷ a N i / u | *i t t i / u |
| PM (modified) | *N a N i  k u | *i xʷ a N i k u | *i t t i k u |

type of final in the two protolanguages together with a possible modification of the PM reconstruction in the light of the PA evidence. The hypothesis is only a hypothesis, however, and has not

work by Stanley Newman, Morris Swadesh, Sarah Gudschinsky, and other scholars cited therein. In a more recent paper ("On linguistic affinities of Amuzgo", *IJAL*, 32.46.9 [1966]) Longacre summarizes the results of some of this work in the following terms: "Detailed comparative work has been done within the Mixtecan, Popolocan and Chiapanec-Manguean language families. It has further been demonstrated that these three families are related. Gudschinsky's initial coupling of Mixtecan and Popolocan has been more recently amplified and brought into sharper focus. Amuzgo itself has been worked into the reconstructions. By now we can with considerable confidence offer (1) a sketch of the phonological structure of reconstructed Popolocan-Mixtecan-Amuzgoan (and probably including Chiapanec-Manguean); (2) a phonological characterization of Proto-Mixtecan as a descendant of this earlier layer; and (3) a phonological characterization of Proto-Popolocan as another descendant of this earlier layer."
[22]   This is a term used by Longacre and others in the works mentioned.
[23]   Mary R. Haas, "A new linguistic relationship in North America: Algonkian and the Gulf languages", *Southwestern Journal of Anthropology*, 14.231-64 (1958).

yet been verified.[24] It is shown as an example of the way in which a new insight in regard to the reconstruction in one protolanguage may be gained through comparison with another protolanguage.


## 2.5 PROBLEMS OF MORPHOLOGICAL RECONSTRUCTION


### 2.51 *How morphological change differs from phonological change*

Each time the reconstruction of a new linguistic family is undertaken, the comparativist is struck anew with the beautiful regularity of the phonological correspondences to be found among the daughter languages. Even though there are almost always some phonological loose ends, the over-all consistency of the system is generally sufficient to give him renewed confidence in the comparative method. But once he turns his attention to the problems of morphological reconstruction, the terrain becomes much more difficult and he is well-advised to proceed with the utmost caution. It is here that he will find whole systems (say the paradigmatic structure of the verb) being simplified in one language, elaborated in another language, and completely rearranged in still another language. While it is true that he will still follow the same basic ground rule, namely to set up as the prototype system the simplest one ADEQUATE to explain the divergent developments of the daughter

---

[24] Verification will include seeing how this gibes with other special developments of *VkV, as discussed in 2.2. Developments of the type there include *aki*, *aka*, *iki*, and *uku*; no certain examples of *iku* have been found. A caution must be inserted at this point, however. If this new hypothesis is the answer, it has to be a development which is chronologically earlier than the type described in 2.2. Otherwise Choctaw would have final *ik* and Koas. final *i* in the words for 'fish', 'squirrel', and 'tree' (see Table II) in parallel fashion with the words for 'day', 'night', etc. Since the development is not parallel, it can be fitted into the scheme ONLY by assuming that it took place BEFORE the other changes affecting *VkV. If this hypothesis turns out to be untenable in its present form, this does not invalidate the principal point being illustrated here, namely that the comparison of two protolanguages may suggest a modification of certain reconstructions in one or the other or both of them. It only means that a modification different from that shown in Table V will have to be worked out.

languages, the whole process is much more complicated than the
setting up of a phonological system which can be verified with
multiple examples of the same sound correspondence, or, frequently
enough, patterned sets of sound correspondences (e.g. 'Grimm's
law'). Phonological systems can be set up by working backwards
to the protolanguage and checked by working forward to the
daughter languages. Paradigmatic and inflectional systems, however, are often affected first by phonological change and then by
analogic loss or re-formation (leveling) so that the end results in
the various daughter languages may give the impression of having
very little in common. If the analogical leveling has been extensive
enough, it will not be possible to find the solution by making a
conventional phonological reconstruction of each term in a paradigm.[25] Instead it may be necessary to make a series of hypotheses
about the structure of the paradigm as a whole until a model is
arrived at which comes nearest to explaining what is actually found
in each of the daughter languages.

### 2.52 *A model for the Muskogean verbal system*

The prototype verbal paradigm of the Muskogean languages
provides an interesting example.[26] In all of the Muskogean languages the third person subject of the active verbal paradigm is an
unmarked category. The marked categories are first and second
person singular and plural (symbolized as 1S, 2S, 1P, and 2P). In
Choctaw the 1S element is a suffix and the other three elements are
prefixes, whereas in Hitchiti and Creek all the elements are suffixes;
see Table VI.

    If these were the only three Muskogean languages for which
materials were available, we could, on the basis of the evidence
shown in Table VI, construct three hypotheses: (1) the protosystem
was like Choctaw, but Hitchiti and Creek have leveled out the
position of the affixes to agree with the suffixed first person; (2) the

[25]  Cf. also Calvert Watkins, "Remarks on reconstruction and historical
linguistic method", *Indo-European origins of the Celtic verb*, 1-8 (Dublin, 1962).
[26]  Mary R. Haas, "A Proto-Muskogean paradigm", *Lg.*, 22. 326-32 (1946).

protosystem was like Hitchiti and Creek, but Choctaw has 'inno-
vated' a prefixed position for the 2S, 1P, and 2P affixes; (3) the
protosystem had two classes of paradigms, one like Choctaw, the
other like Hitchiti and Creek. Without further evidence, many
workers would probably prefer the first hypothesis, since it seems
somehow 'simpler'. The third hypothesis would probably be least

TABLE VI
*Subject affixes of Choctaw, Hitchiti, and Creek*

|  | CHOCTAW Prefix    Suffix | | HITCHITI Suffix | CREEK Suffix |
|---|---|---|---|---|
| S1 | | -li | -li | -ay- |
| 2 | iš- | | -icka | -ick- |
| P1 | il-; i·-/C | | -i·ka | -iy-; -i·-/C |
| 2 | haš- | | -a·cka | -a·ck- |

favored since it is, on the face of it, simply additive and, in this
form at least, does not seem to 'explain' anything. As will be
brought out in the ensuing discussion, the third hypothesis is best
on the Proto-Muskogean level and the first hypothesis can only be
made workable at the pre-Proto-Muskogean level.

Fortunately, Choctaw, Hitchiti, and Creek are not the only
Muskogean languages for which paradigmatic material is available,
and still more fortunately, the material from the additional source
is of such a nature as to solve the problem. Whereas Choctaw,
Hitchiti, and Creek have a single paradigmatic class each, Koasati
has a total of three paradigmatic classes, the first of which is
identical with the single Choctaw paradigm, and the third of which
closely resembles the single Hitchiti paradigm, while Creek shows
only slight phonological variations of the latter; see Table VII.
That the three-class system of Koasati is a reflection of certain important features of the Proto-Muskogean system is attested by the
fact that it shows the framework within which the difference
between the Choctaw system, on the one hand, and the Hitchiti and
Creek systems, on the other, could have originated; see Table VIII.
Furthermore, a careful study of the various uses of Classes II and

TABLE VII

*Koasati subject affixes*

|  | CLASS I Prefix Suffix | CLASS IIA, B CLASS IIC Infix (suff.) Suffix Infix Suffix | CLASS III Suffix |
|---|---|---|---|
| S1 | -li | -li          -li | -li |
| 2 | is- | -ci(-)         -ci- | -(h)iska |
| P1 | il- | -hili(-)        -li- | -(h)ilka |
| 2 | has- | -haci(-)        -haci- | -(h)aska |

III in Koasati helps provide the clue to the probable origin of these classes. Even though the chief evidence comes entirely from Koasati, it is possible to construct a model of the pre-Proto-Muskogean paradigm[27] which requires only one set of subject affixes (basically those of Class I, Table VIII, with slightly varying allomorphs for some affixes) and two classes of verb stems,[28] (1)

TABLE VIII

*Proto-Muskogean Subject affixes*

|  | CLASS I Prefix    Suffix | CLASS II Infix (suff.)  Suffix | CLASS III Suffix |
|---|---|---|---|
| S1 | *-li | *-li | *-kali |
| 2 | *iš- | *-ši- | *-iška |
| P1 | *il(i)- | *-hili- | *-(h)ilika |
| 2 | *haš(i)- | *-haši- | *-(h)aš(i)ka |

those to which the subject affixes are attached directly, and (2) those which are conjugated only periphrastically with the subject affixes

---

[27]  The development of this hypothesis, as described here, is new and not to be found in my earlier paper "A Proto-Muskogean paradigm".

[28]  Or, alternatively, two methods of conjugating verbs. The hypothesis of two classes of verb stems implies that SOME verb stems were inflected one way and OTHER verb stems were inflected the other way. This seems the most likely hypothesis, but the other possibility, namely that in the pre-Proto-Muskogean period all, or at least many, verb stems could be conjugated both ways, cannot be ruled out entirely.

being attached to the auxiliary verb stem and the whole thing added to the main verb stem; see Table IX.[29]

TABLE IX

*Model of pre-Proto-Muskogean verbal conjugation*

| Direct conjugation of verb stem (VS) | | Conjugation of auxiliaries Aux. 1 (LI) | | Aux. 2 (KA) | |
|---|---|---|---|---|---|
| S1 | | VS li | VS + | LI li | VS + | KA li |
| 2 | iš | VS | VS + ši | LI | VS + (h)iš | KA |
| 3 | | VS | VS + | LI | VS + | KA |
| P1 | ili | VS | VS + (hi)li | LI | VS + (h)ili | KA |
| 2 | haš | VS | VS + haši | LI | VS + (h)aš | KA |

It might reasonably be asked why the model shown in Table IX is assigned to the pre-Proto-Muskogean period rather than to the Proto-Muskogean period. In the Proto-Muskogean period the auxiliaries symbolized as LI and KA in Table IX had already developed into classifying suffixes, *-li* as a transitivizer and *-ka* as a mediopassive. Analogical leveling in Choctaw resulted in a simple conjugational system wherein subject affixes descended from PM Class I (Table VIII) were used with ALL verb stems, including those containing -li and -a (the Choctaw equivalents of PM *-li* and *-ka*, respectively). Hitchiti and Creek, on the other hand, use as their ONLY subject affixes ONLY those forms (Class III of Table VIII) which have originated from a complete amalgamation of the prototype subject affixes with Auxiliary Verb 2 (KA in Table IX). This means that ALL verb stems, including those containing descendants of *-li* (H -li, C -y-) and *-ka* (H -ka, C -k-) are conjugated with what originally belonged only to *-ka* verbs. Hitchiti verbs in -ka and Creek verbs in -k- thus contain two morphs -ka or -k-; both

[29] In Table IX the following special abbreviations are used: VS, verb stem; LI, stem of the first auxiliary verb (now retained in some languages as -li, classifying suffix of transitive verbs); and KA, stem of the second auxiliary verb (now retained in some languages as -ka, classifying suffix of certain intransitive verbs). The shape of the third person form, even here an unmarked category, is included in the table in order to show the relationship between verb stem and auxiliary when no subject affix is used. Spaces are used in all three columns of the table to indicate morph boundaries.

are ultimately from the same source (i.e. were identical) but through reinterpretation and analogical leveling they now have completely different functions. Choctaw, Hitchiti, and Creek paradigms illustrating this are shown in Table X.[30]

TABLE X

*Choctaw, Hitchiti, and Creek paradigms of* *-li *and* *-ka *verbs*

|  | CHOCTAW | HITCHITI | CREEK |
|---|---|---|---|
| *-li* | kul.li 'to dig' | patap.li- 'to hit' | wana.y- 'to tie' |
| verbs S1 | KUL.LI li | PATAP.LI li- | WANA.Y ay- |
| 2 | iš KUL.LI | PATAP.L icka- | WANA.Y ick- |
| 3 | KUL.LI | PATAP.LI | WANA.Y- |
| P1 | i· KUL.LI | PATAP.L i·ka- | WANA.Y iy-(i·/C) |
| 2 | haš KUL.LI | PATAP.L a·cka- | WANA.Y a·ck- |
| *-ka* | pū·fa 'to blow' | pu·f.ka- 'to blow' | pu·f.k- 'to blow' |
| verbs S1 | PŪ·F.A li | PU·F.KA li- | PU·F.K ay- |
| 2 | iš PŪ·F.A | PU·F.K icka- | PU·F.K ick- |
| 3 | PŪ·F.A | PU·F.KA- | PU·F.K- |
| P1 | i· PŪ·F.A | PU·F.K i·ka- | PU·F.K iy- (i·/C) |
| 2 | haš PŪ·F.A | PU·F.K a·cka- | PU·F.K a·ck- |

Koasati is the one language which has reflexes of all three Proto-Muskogean classes of Table VIII (from the three conjugation types of Table IX), but it too has undergone some very special kinds of development. These are shown in Table XI and may be described as follows: (1) Some, but not all, plain Koasati verb stems (i.e. those lacking the classifying suffixes -li and -ka or the causative suffix -ci) which end in ..V(·)CV belong to Class I. (2) Class II includes all verbs with the classifying suffix -li (or an allomorph), but the suffix appears ONLY before 1S -li and in the third person, which is unmarked for subject. In addition Class II includes all

---

[30] In Table X an actual verb stem is used as an example. It is shown in capital letters with a period indicating the boundary between root and classifying suffix. As in Table IX spaces are used to show the boundaries between the verb stem and its subject affixes.

stems ending in ..VCCV (e.g. *huhcá* 'to dig').[31] (3) Class III includes
all stems ending in ..*kV*, i.e. ..*ka*, ..*ki*, and ..*ku*, but the -*kV*
appears only before 1S -*li* and in the third person, which is unmarked for subject. This means that all Koasati verbs ending in
..*kV* are conjugated as if they were old *-*ka* verbs (see 'to chew' in
Table XI as the model with KA in capital letters), but the simplest
synchronic interpretation is that the 2S, 1P, and 2P prefixes have
been amalgamated with the old *-*ka* to give Class III affixes (see 'to
pay', 'to drink', and 'to teach' in Table XI). That this is indeed the
simplest synchronic interpretation is seen in the fact that Class III
also includes certain stems lacking ..*kV*, viz. all those ending in
the causative suffix -*ci* (except when -*ci* is preceded by transitivizing
-*li* which automatically places them in Class II).

TABLE XI

*Koasati paradigms of Classes I, II, and III including* *li *and* *-ka *verbs*

| CLASS I | | CLASS IIA | CLASS IIB | CLASS IIC | |
|---|---|---|---|---|---|
| | | (-*li* verbs) | | | |
| | hica 'to see' | kalas.li | buk.li.ci | huhca 'to dig' | |
| | | 'to scratch' | 'to thresh' | | |
| S1 | HICA li | KALAS LI li | BUK LI CI li | HU | HCA li |
| 2 | is HICA | KALAS ci Ø | BUK ci Ø CI | HU ci | HCA |
| 3 | HICA | KALAS LI | BUK LI CI | HU | HCA |
| P1 | il HICA | KALAS hili Ø | BUK hili Ø CI | HU li | HCA |
| 2 | has HICA | KALAS haci Ø | BUK haci Ø CI | HU haci HCA | |

| CLASS IIIA | | | CLASS IIIB | |
|---|---|---|---|---|
| (-*ka* verb) | (other -*kV* verbs) | | | |
| | yas.ka | imfi·ki | isku | impunna.ci |
| | 'to chew' | 'to pay' | 'to drink' | 'to teach' |
| S1 | YAS KA li | IMFI·KI li | ISKU li | IMPUNNA.CI li |
| 2 | YAS is KA | IMFI· hiska | IS iska | IMPUNNA.C iska |
| 3 | YAS KA | IMFI·KI | ISKU | IMPUNNA.CI |
| P1 | YAS il KA | IMFI· hilka | IS ilka | IMPUNNA.C ilka |
| 2 | YAS as KA | IMFI· haska | IS aska | IMPUNNA.C aska |

[31] Class II also includes a very few stems, such as *tala* 'to weave', which do not
fit either category and which, by canonical shape, one would expect to belong
to Class I. This is a clear example of the arbitrariness of the class system at
present.

This concludes the discussion of the development of the Proto-Muskogean conjugational system of the active verb in the extant daughter languages. The pre-Proto-Muskogean model in Table IX provides an example of 'internal reconstruction' within a proto-language and its value as a means of explaining the extant systems has been well demonstrated. Its further value as a model to be used in deeper comparisons is discussed in 3.2.

# 3. THE RANKING OF PROTOLANGUAGES AND PROBLEMS OF COMPARISON AT DEEPER LEVELS

## 3.1 ORDERS OF PROTOLANGUAGES

### 3.11 *Comparing protolanguages*

When phonological reconstructions of a large number of etyma are available in two or more protolanguages it is possible to compare these to determine whether or not the protolanguages may be sister languages and hence daughter languages of a still earlier proto-language. This type of comparison is of crucial importance for scholars working on languages which lack ancient written records. Since we do not have and shall never have records of ancient Algonkian, Muskogean, Siouan, Iroquoian, Athapaskan, and a host of others, we have no choice but first to compare sister languages in order to reconstruct the protolanguage for each family. If this is properly done these protolanguages can serve us almost as well in our attempts to make deeper comparisons as ancient written languages like Latin, Greek, Sanskrit, and Hittite have served our Indo-European confreres. Anyone who denigrates the work of reconstructing such protolanguages is actually expressing distrust of the comparative method itself.[1] The fact that Proto-Romance turns out to be a kind of Latin is precisely the sort of thing that serves as a check on the validity of our methods. I have not heard of anyone wanting to throw out Proto-Germanic because there are no written records of the Germanic of the time to substantiate it.

---

[1] This is not to say that every body of starred forms has been arrived at in strict accordance with the comparative method. But if not it is due to the ineptitude of the worker or to the fragmentary nature of his material.

Nor do I believe for a moment that scholars would have found themselves unable to reconstruct Proto-Indo-European without written records. In view of the large numbers of living languages belonging to this family, one cannot believe that the interrelationships would have gone undetected and that methods to deal with them would have remained undeveloped. Or, for those who can think of the discovery of the interrelationship of the Indo-European languages only in terms of the way in which it actually took place, let us put it this way. If the comparative method had been developed in respect to another family of languages (say Semitic or Sino-Tibetan), comparativists would have by now been able to work out the interrelationships of living Indo-European languages even if there were no records earlier than 1800 A.D. The possibility of discovering genetic relationships, then, does not stand or fall on the basis of the presence or absence of ancient documents. Reconstructed protolanguages can and do take the place of ancient records when the latter are unavailable.

As we continue to refine our methods of comparing proto-languages,[2] it may turn out to be desirable to use a special terminology to describe different ranks of protolanguages. Elsewhere I have proposed that we speak of protolanguages of the FIRST ORDER and of the SECOND ORDER.[3] A protolanguage of the first order is one reconstructed from natural languages, written or unwritten. A protolanguage of the second order is then one reconstructed on the basis of two or more protolanguages of the first order. Deeper ranks, as of the third order or more, can be added as needed.

### 3.12 The problem of language isolates

It turns out that some natural languages are orphans, that is, they have no known sister languages with which they can be compared in order to participate in the reconstruction of a protolanguage of

---

[2]    Even though it is still the same old comparative method applied at a deeper level, refinements are to be expected in any ongoing science.
[3]    "A new linguistic relationship in North America...", 259.

the first order. I propose to call such languages LANGUAGE ISOLATES.[4] Their genealogical classification can be determined, if at all, only by comparing them with protolanguages of the first order or even of the second order or more. When this has been done and a body of reconstructions has been painstakingly worked out, what we have is not an expanded or stretched out protolanguage of the first order, but a protolanguage of the second order. This is a point of considerable methodological significance and one which is again and again misunderstood, even by linguists. For example, the Natchez language (formerly spoken near the present Natchez, Mississippi) is a language isolate. It has been suggested that it is related to the Muskogean languages.[5] If this is so, Natchez is NOT the sister language of Choctaw, Koasati, Hitchiti, and Creek but is a COLLATERAL[6] of Proto-Muskogean itself and possibly of other protolanguages and language isolates (see Table XII)[7]. Further

[4] I first used the term in a paper entitled "Is Kutenai related to Algonkian?" read at the Conference on Indigenous Languages in North America held at the University of Alberta in July, 1964. The term is intended to be a technical one and was constructed by inverting the phrase ISOLATED LANGUAGES, long in use as a descriptive, if not technical, term for such languages. For example, Whitney uses the phrase 'isolated tongues' (in the text) or 'isolated languages' (in the running head) in *Language and the study of language'*, 355 (New York, 1875).
[5] This was apparently first discussed in detail by John R. Swanton in "The Muskhogean connection of the Natchez language", *IJAL*, 3.46-75 (1924). A more recent treatment of the problem is by Mary R. Haas in "Natchez and the Muskogean languages", *Lg.*, 32.61-72 (1956).
[6] It is not correct to say that Natchez is a sister language of Proto-Muskogean; instead it is the sole known descendant of an ancestor language contemporaneous with Proto-Muskogean. Such an ancestor language is, however, unknowable and for this reason is also not to be termed a sister language of Proto-Muskogean. To get around the difficulty I prefer to say that Natchez, if related, is a 'collateral' of Proto-Muskogean since both would be descended from the same protolanguage of the second order.
[7] As suggested in my "A new linguistic relationship...". Special abbreviations used are PL$^1$, PL$^2$, and PL$^3$ for protolanguage of the first order, second order, and third order. Language abbreviations are: Alg., Algonkian; Wiy., Wiyot; Yur., Yurok; Atak., Atakapa; Chit., Chitimacha; Tun., Tunica; Nat., Natchez; Musk., Muskogean; PA, Proto-Algonkian; PM, Proto-Muskogean. On the far left of the table are time estimates. All are impressionistic, but it should be remembered that PA and PM show a kind of divergence similar to what is familiar to us in the Romance and Germanic families of languages.

refinements of the interrelationships among languages included in a construct such as that shown in Table XII cannot be stated until a vast amount of phonological and morphological comparison has been carried out. The methods of phonological comparison are more or less the traditional ones; some of these are illustrated in section 3.3. More challenging is the problem of finding methods of undertaking morphological comparison. This is discussed in the immediately following section.

TABLE XII

*A preliminary model of Wiyot-Yurok-Algonkian-Gulf interrelationships*

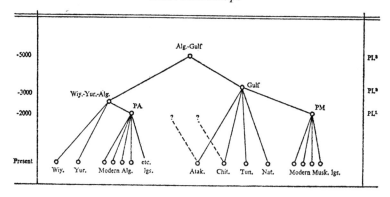

## 3.2 THE COMPARISON OF PARADIGMATIC MODELS

It has already been demonstrated that even within such a close-knit family as the Muskogean it is not possible to reconstruct the prototype paradigmatic structure of the active verb by means of ordinary phonological reconstruction alone. But the problem need not be abandoned on this account. Instead, as has been shown for Proto-Muskogean and pre-Proto-Muskogean, one can attempt to construct a deductive model of the protosystem and if the end results found in the daughter languages can be successfully explained by its use, its utility will have been demonstrated.

The question then arises: Can anything significant ever be observed by comparing a paradigmatic model constructed for one protolanguage with that of another protolanguage, or with that of a language isolate suspected of being a collateral language? The answer would seem to depend on whether or not the two models being compared can be seen to share some unique or unexpected feature, or perhaps some asymmetrical feature which might be considered diagnostic of possible genetic relationship. As shown in Table XII, there are four language isolates which are thought to be related to Proto-Muskogean, namely, Natchez, Tunica, Chitimacha, and Atakapa.[8] Of these both Natchez and Tunica can combine active verb stems with conjugated auxiliaries to form periphrastic paradigms. Natchez conjugates its auxiliaries by means of subject prefixes for the first, second, and third persons, and the third person is a marked, not an unmarked category. The resemblance between the Natchez model and the pre-Proto-Muskogean model of Table IX is thus general and on the whole rather vague. There is nothing here to indicate that the models could not be developed from the same prototype but at the same time there is nothing to strike one as particularly diagnostic of relationship.

The equivalent model for Tunica, however, tells a different story. In Table XIII a part of the pre-Proto-Muskogean model of Table IX is laid out alongside the Tunica model of periphrastic conjugation based on the auxiliary -hki ($\sim$ ʔahki- $\sim$ ʔaki) meaning 'is'. Tunica has proliferated the model by making gender distinctions (M, masculine; F, feminine) in the second and third persons. Aside from this the asymmetrical features of the pre-Proto-Muskogean model are duplicated exactly: (1) the first person subject morph is suffixed (*-li in pre-PM, -ni in Tunica), (2) the second person subject morph is prefixed, and (3) the third person is an unmarked category (provided the Tunica third person singular feminine form is taken as being older).[9]

---

[8]  These are the so-called 'Gulf' languages. Tunica was formerly spoken along the Yazoo River in Mississippi (later along the Red River in central Louisiana); Chitimacha was spoken near the mid coastal area of Louisiana and Atakapa along the western coastal area of the same state.

[9]  Its lack of symmetry guarantees that the 3FS form is older while the 3MS is clearly a re-formation on the analogy of the second person forms.

TABLE XIII

*Comparison of pre-Muskogean and Tunica models of periphrastic conjugation with an auxiliary and its subject affixes*

| PRE-PROTO-MUSKOGEAN Periphrastic conjugation with *-ka Aux. | | | | TUNICA Periphrastic conjugation with -hki Aux. | | | |
|---|---|---|---|---|---|---|---|
| | Prefix | Suffix | | | Prefix | Suffix | |
| S1 | VS + | KA | li | S1 | VS + | ʔAHKI | ni |
| 2 | VS + (h)iš KA | | | 2M | VS + wi HKI | | |
| | | | | 2F | VS + hi HKI | | |
| 3 | | | | 3M | VS + ʔu HKI | | |
| | VS + | KA | | 3F | VS + | ʔAKI | |

This example of the comparison of paradigmatic models has been given, not to 'prove' that Tunica and Proto-Muskogean are genetically related, but to show the utility of models of this sort for morphological comparison and reconstruction. 'Proof' of relationship, on the other hand, needs not only this kind of evidence but lexical evidence as well. Moreover, one cannot expect that the comparison of morphological models will always be as rewarding as it is in the case of Proto-Muskogean and Tunica. The functionally equivalent Natchez model, even though it could very easily be a derivative of, say, a model like the Tunica one,[10] has, if related, leveled out (or 'regularized') its conjugational system until it no longer contains any special feature or combination of features of diagnostic usefulness. However, whenever special features are uncovered by the use of such models, their utility is not to be doubted. In the case of unwritten languages, such as those illustrated, such evidence can be priceless, but so far as I know this type of comparison among unwritten languages has been almost entirely unexploited. It is to be hoped that the Muskogean and Tunica example will serve as an incentive to others to try out the method in other language families.

---

[10]   A complete model of the conjugation of auxiliary verbs in Natchez would, if placed alongside a similarly complete model of those in Tunica, show a great many points of similarity.

### 3.3 THE STRATEGY OF PHONOLOGICAL COMPARISON AT DEEPER LEVELS

When Sapir presented materials in 1913 intended to show that Wiyot and Yurok are genetically related to the Algonkian family (see the lefthand portion of Table XII), his hypothesis received acceptance in some quarters but in general was met with disbelief.[11] Among the factors contributing to the lack of acceptance were several which could be expected to be mitigated or remedied with the passage of time, viz., (1) many people were not yet ready to accept any deeper relationships among the chronologically shallow linguistic families of North America as set up by Powell,[12] (2) the available records of both Wiyot and Yurok were not only scanty but poor, and (3) the sound correspondences among the Algonkian languages themselves were either unknown or inadequately understood.[13] A few cultural anthropologists like Dixon and Kroeber were themselves engaged in postulating deeper relationships and hence were inclined to be favorably disposed toward Sapir's proposal.[14] The leading Algonkianists of the time, on the other hand, had been trained in the rigorous methodology of Indo-European linguistics (as had Sapir) and they could not accept Sapir's con-

[11] Edward Sapir, "Wiyot and Yurok, Algonkin languages of California", *American Anthropologist*, n.s., 13.617-646 (1913). Debated by Truman Michelson in "Two alleged Algonquian Languages of California", *American Anthropologist*, n.s., 16.361-67 (1914).

[12] John W. Powell, "Indian linguistic families of America north of Mexico", *Seventh Annual Report of the Bureau of [American] Ethnology*, 7.7-142 (1891).

[13] The first complete statement of these sound correspondences was based on a selection of the Central Algonkian languages only and was presented a dozen years later by Bloomfield in "On the sound-system of Central Algonquian" (1.5, footnote 15); see also sections 1.4. and 1.5.

[14] Roland B. Dixon and A. L. Kroeber, "Linguistic families of California", *UCPAAE*, 16.47-118 (1919). "The authors therefore accept his [Sapir's] findings in full confidence..." (113). But some felt otherwise. Franz Boas, in particular, was completely skeptical of Sapir's proposal even after Gladys Reichard's fuller material on Wiyot became available. It is well known, of course, that in his later years Boas was skeptical of all attempts to find deeper relationships among the American Indian languages. See, for example, his "The classification of American languages", *American Anthropologist*, n.s., 22.367-76 (1920). Further discussion of the reason for Boas's view is given in 5.21.

clusion without a stricter marshalling of sound correspondences than Sapir could manage with the type of material at his disposal.[15] Complete acceptance of the hypothesis was consequently withheld for almost fifty years since it was obvious that there would always be a lingering doubt until the Algonkianists were brought around.

The major difficulty lay in having to treat Wiyot and Yurok as sister languages of Cree, Ojibwa, Fox, Natick, Micmac, etc., for it is now clear that the best way of tackling the problem is to operate with Proto-Algonkian as a protolanguage of the first order and to compare Wiyot and Yurok with this rather than with the various Algonkian daughter languages individually as Sapir had been obliged to do.[16]

I have chosen Yurok and Proto-Algonkian to serve as an illustration of the comparison of a collateral language and a protolanguage.[17] Proto-Algonkian probably has a time depth of around two millennia and when we compare it (rather than Cree, Ojibwa, etc.) with Yurok we have advantages of almost the same quality as when we compare Latin (rather than French, Portuguese, etc.) with, say, Gothic (assuming we did not yet have Proto-Germanic). It is maintained (3.11) that a protolanguage reconstructed on the basis of a group of contemporary unwritten languages can serve us almost as well in arriving at deeper relationships as can an ancient written language of comparable antiquity. In corroboration of this

[15]  Truman Michelson attempted to refute Sapir's proposal in "Two alleged Algonquian languages of California", *American Anthropologist*, n.s., 16.361-67 (1914). C. C. Uhlenbeck also expressed skepticism in several places, e.g. "Review of A. Meillet et M. Cohen, *Les langues du monde* ..., 1924", *IJAL*, 4.114-6 (1927).
[16]  Sapir was hampered methodologically by the lack of Proto-Algonkian reconstructions. Nevertheless, he recognized the probable nature of the relationship for he said: "Whether Wiyot and Yurok, and Algonkin proper are three distinct major divisions of the stock remains to be seen"; "Wiyot and Yurok ...", 646.
[17]  See also my "Algonkian-Ritwan: the end of a controversy", *IJAL*, 24.159-73 (1958) where both Wiyot and Yurok are compared with PA. 'Ritwan' is a term used by Dixon and Kroeber to refer to Wiyot and Yurok as a stock; see "Linguistic families...", 112-3. A recently published paper comparing the two California languages is that of Karl V. Teeter, "Wiyot and Yurok: a preliminary study", *Studies in Californian linguistics*, ed. William Bright (= *UCPL*, 34), 192-8 (1964).

contention we present in Table XIV a sample set of eleven cognates between Proto-Algonkian and Yurok.[18]

TABLE XIV

Algonkian and Yurok cognates

| | 1. his brain | 2. his mouth | 3. his tooth | 4. knee | 5. winter |
|---|---|---|---|---|---|
| Sh | hotep-i | hoto·n-i | wi·pit-i /wi·pici/ | —— | pepo·n |
| C | otihp-i | oto·n | wi·pit | -kitik | pipo·n |
| O | wi(ni)ntip | oto·n | wi·pit; -a·pit- (med.) | -kitikw- | pepo·n |
| D | wtəmp- | wtú·n | wípit | kətkw- | —— |
| PA | *wetemp-i ~ *wentep-i | *weto·n-i | *wi·pit-i; *-a·pit- | *-ketekw | *pepo·n- |
| Y | 'his hair' we?lep | welul | werpel | (?ə)kəl | kipu·n |

| | 6. turn | 7.long (sg.) | 8.long (pl.) | 9. bone | 10.his liver | 11. his tail (bird) |
|---|---|---|---|---|---|---|
| Sh | piyem- | kinw- | kaka·nw- | ho?kan-i | —— | —— |
| C | pi·m | kin- | —— | oskan | oskon | otani |
| O | pi·m- | ken- | kaka·n- | ikkan | okko·n | ——; M wana·ny |
| D | pim- | —— | —— | waxkan | oxkwən- | —— |
| PA | *pyem- | *kenw- | *kaka·nw- | *waθkan- | *weθk-wan-i | *waθany-i |
| Y | kelom- | knew- | kokonew | wəlkə? | wəlkun | wələy 'tail' (not bird) |

The examples illustrate sound correspondences of the same type that would be found in comparing any two cognate languages. Aside from identical correspondences (*p : p, *k : k, *m : m, etc.) there are several which are nonidentical:

[18] The abbreviations used in Table XIV are as follows: Sh, Shawnee; C, Cree; O, Ojibwa; D, Delaware; M, Menomini; PA, Proto-Algonkian; Y, Yurok. The inanimate singular suffix -i is always separated by a hyphen in the forms quoted. The PA vowels are *i *e *a *o (short and long); consonants are *p *t *c *k *s *š *h *θ *l *m *n *w *y. Additional symbols used in Delaware are ə (schwa), u (short and long), and x (voiceless velar spirant). The Yurok vowels are i e ə (retroflex 'er') a o u (short and long); consonants p t c k k^w (also glottalized p' etc.) s š l g (voiced velar spirant) h l r m n w y ?; see R. H. Robins, The Yurok language (= UCPL, 15), 1-300 (1958). Some of the comparisons shown in Table XIV appear also in my "Algonkian-Ritwan ..." but 'turn' (no. 6) and 'long (pl.)' (no. 8) are new and for 'winter' (no. 5) a better PA cognate has been found.

*t   :  *l, l* in 'his brain' (Y 'his hair), 'his mouth', 'his tooth', 'knee'.

*θ   :  *l* in 'his tail'.

*θk  :  *lk* in 'bone', 'his liver'. (The symbol *θ in *θk is formulaic only and is not to be equated with *θ in other positions in spite of the seeming similar correspondent in Y.)

*n   :  *l* in 'his mouth' (3rd C).

*y   :  *l* in 'turn'.

*p   :  *k* in 'winter' (1st C), 'turn'.

*an  :  *ə* (except after *kw*) in 'bone', 'his tail'. Preceding *ə* is harmonizing.

Forms from some of the daughter languages of Algonkian are also shown in Table XIV in order to illustrate the point that it is usually easier to compare Yurok with PA than it is with one of the daughter languages. For example, most of the nonidentical correspondences listed above show a Yurok reflex of *l* or *l* and the PA correspondent is *t, *θ, *n, or *y. But Cree has *t* < PA *t and *θ and *y* < PA *l and *y; Ojibwa has *n* < PA *n, *l, *θ; Shawnee has *l* < PA *l and *θ. Under the circumstances it is simpler to work out the Yurok correspondences in relation to PA. Indeed Sapir ran into difficulties on this account since the PA reconstructions had not been worked out at the time he proposed the Wiyot-Yurok-Algonkian relationship. Observe the following comment:[19]

> ...Cree sometimes has *t* where Ojibwa and Fox have *n*. ... in practically all such cases Eastern dialects have *l*, so that what is really involved is not primarily a *t* — *n* interchange but a *t* — *l* interchange. Here again Wiyot and Yurok are confirmatory, inasmuch as they sometimes have *l* where Algonkian has *t* or vice versa.

We now know that when Cree *t* corresponds to Ojibwa, Fox *n* and Eastern *l* the PA reconstruction is *θ. But immediately following this remark Sapir gives examples of Wiyot *l* corresponding to Cree, Ojibwa, Fox, etc. *t*, all of which reflect PA *t. One of his examples is Wiyot *walul* 'his mouth' (see Y and PA in Table XIV). It is obvious that this kind of confusion can be avoided only when reconstructed forms are available. On the other hand, it is im-

---

[19] Sapir, "Wiyot and Yurok...", 641.

portant to observe that even though Sapir's examples did not happen to illustrate his comment, he was essentially right. See 'his tail' (Table XIV) where PA *$\theta$ : Y *l*.

### 3.4 MORPHOLOGICAL COMPARISON AT DEEPER LEVELS

This can reveal similarities, dissimilarities, or some of both. If only dissimilarities are revealed, the relationship is assumed to be more remote than when at least some similarities are brought to light. An excellent example of a remarkable set of similarities is seen in the inflection of inalienably possessed nouns[20] in Proto-Algonkian as compared with that in the collateral languages, Wiyot and Yurok (see Table XV).[21]

TABLE XV
*Possessive paradigms of Wiyot, Yurok, and Algonkian*

| | my tooth, etc. | | | my mouth, etc. | | |
|---|---|---|---|---|---|---|
| | Wiyot | Yurok | PA | Wiyot | Yurok | PA |
| 1 | *d*-ápt | *n*-erpeł | *\*n-i·pit-* | [ka]-lùl | *ne*-luł | *\*ne-to·n-* |
| 2 | *kh*-ápt | *k'*-erpeł | *\*k-i·pit-* | *kha*-lùl | *k'e*-luł | *\*ke-to·n-* |
| 3 | *w*-apt-áhl | *w*-erpeł | *\*w-i·pit-* | *wa*-lul-àhl | *we*-luł | *\*we-to·n-* |
| 4 | *b*-apt | *m*-erpeł | *\*m-i·pit-* | *ba*-lùl | *me*-luł | *\*me-to·n-* |

Proto-Algonkian has a set of four pronominal prefixes for different persons, first person (1), second person (2), third person (3), and a fourth person (4) which indicates a nonspecific or indefinite person (somebody, anybody).[22] Cognate forms of these prefixes occur

[20] 'Inalienably possessed' nouns are those which occur only in combination with possessive elements (usually prefixes or suffixes). Such nouns are normally body-part or kinship terms. Other nouns are said to be 'alienably possessed', i.e. they may be used either with or without possessive elements.
[21] The following works are the sources for the material provided in the table: Leonard Bloomfield, "Algonquian"; Karl V. Teeter, *The Wiyot Language* (= *UCPL*, 37), 1-251 (1964); R. H. Robins, *The Yurok Language*.
[22] This person is used when it is not necessary to specify the possessor. It also indicates the indefinite, e.g. 'a tooth'. In Yurok its use with body-parts indicates that the part has been separated from the body, as in butchering.

also in Wiyot and Yurok in an identically structured closed set of four. The only noncognate form is Wiyot *ka-*, enclosed in brackets, in [*ka*]-*lùl* 'my mouth'. Aside from this not only the prefixes but also the stems are cognate in all the languages. (The third person forms for PA and Yurok are also to be found in Table XIV). The Wiyot suffix -*ahl* in the third person forms is cognate with PA *-*ali*, obviative suffix. Kin terms in Algonkian take the obviative in the third person possessed form, e.g. PA *o·hθ-ali* 'his father'. In Wiyot the use of the obviative has been generalized with third person possessive forms.

It must be emphasized that the cognation of the items in Table XV is vouchsafed by similarity in both form and function. Many other languages and language families make use of pronominal prefixes in ways that are very similar to their use in the Algonkian, Wiyot, and Yurok languages, but the actual forms used are phonologically unrelated. Thus in Chipewyan, an Athapaskan language,[23] we find the following set of singular possessive prefixes: *sɛ-* (1), *nɛ-* (2), *bɛ-* (3), *yɛ-* (a second 3rd person in the context), and *ʔɛ-* (indefinite). Broad similarities of this nature are discussed in more detail in chapter 5.

---

[23] Fang-Kuei Li, "Chipewyan", in Harry Hoijer and others, *Linguistic Structures of Native America* (= *Viking Fund Publications in Anthropology*, 6) (New York, 1946).

# 4. PROBLEMS OF CLASSIFICATION

## 4.1 RENEWED INTEREST IN CLASSIFICATION

There has been a definite upsurge of interest in the classificatory and comparative aspects of linguistics in the past 12-15 years. This has led to a renewed interest in the problems of discovering and establishing remote relationships. Consequently there is more activity in more of the languages of the world than ever before. Different linguists specialize in different parts of the world and some, like Morris Swadesh and Joseph Greenberg,[1] work more or less on a global basis. Frequently enough, different linguists, even when they are specializing in more or less the same area come up with varying schemes of interrelationships among the various more remotely connected families and stocks. To outsiders it may seem as if no progress whatever is being made, and some may be inclined to think that the whole thing is meaningless if scholars are not able to reach some kind of agreement on what is related to what and with what degree of closeness. But this kind of disagreement only means that there is much activity in this area of human knowledge.

There is another kind of disagreement among scholars which is

[1] For example, Joseph H. Greenberg, "Studies in African linguistic classification", *Southwestern Journal of Anthropology*, 5.79-100, 190-8, 309-17 (1949), 6.47-63, 143-60, 223-37, 388-98 (1950), and 10.405-15 (1954); *id.*, "The general classification of Central and South American languages", *Selected Papers 5th Internat. Cong. Anthrop. and Ethnol. Sci.*, 791-4 (1960); Morris Swadesh, "Linguistics as an instrument of prehistory", *Southwestern Journal of Anthropology*, 15.20-35 (1959); *id.*, "On interhemisphere linguistic connections", 894-924 in *Culture in history: essays in honor of Paul Radin*, ed. Stanley Diamond (New York, 1960); *id.*, "Linguistic relations across Bering Strait", *American Anthropologist*, 64.262-91 (1962).

more serious, namely the disagreement about methods to be used. But perhaps it is more serious largely because it tends to lead scholars to make extravagant claims for their own methods and at the same time to discredit the methods of others. The simple truth is that all methods have some kind of utility and, further, that some of them have more utility in some kinds of situations than in others.

## 4.2 METHODS OF CLASSIFICATION

### 4.21 *The inspection method*

This involves the inspection of a few hundred words of like meanings culled from a great many languages covering a large geographical area, such as North America, South America, Africa, or Australia, to determine (1) similarities in sound and meaning and (2) dissimilarities in sound and meaning. Languages with many similarities can usually be safely placed together in a single family and those which are dissimilar are separated. The method was used with great success in the early nineteenth century by Albert Gallatin in *A Synopsis of the Indian Tribes within the United States East of the Rocky Mountains and in the British and Russian Possessions in North America.*[2] It was used with equal success in the late nineteenth century by Major Powell and his coworkers in arriving at their definitive statement of the linguistic families of North America north of Mexico.[3]

In the twentieth century the method is still being used with effectiveness whenever a new classificatory hypothesis of relatively shallow time depth is needed. Greenberg, who refers to it as "mass comparison of basic vocabulary,"[4] has used the method in Africa and South America.

[2] *Trans. and Coll. American Antiquarian Soc.*, 2.1-422 (Cambridge, 1836).
[3] John W. Powell, "Indian linguistic families of America north of Mexico", in *Seventh Annual Report of the Bureau of [American] Ethnology*, 7.7-142 (Washington, D.C., 1891).
[4] Joseph H. Greenberg, "Genetic Relationships among Languages", p. 42, in *Essays in Linguistics* (= *Viking Fund Publications in Anthropology*, 24) (New York, 1957).

## 4.22 The method of lexicostatistics

This method, originally called glottochronology, was developed by Swadesh in the early 1950s.[5] In one sense it is a highly condensed variety of the inspection method — condensed because after a certain amount of trial and error a so-called 'diagnostic' list of 100 basic words was arrived at to be used as the basis for inspection. (An alternate list of 100 words could be added if desired.) One great value of the list was that its brevity made possible the collection and assemblage of hundreds of more or less uniform vocabularies for ready comparison.

But the chief importance of lexicostatistics is that it was hoped that it could be used as a method of making a statistical determination of the degree of distance between languages and that the results could then be stated chronologically. Only one kind of change was to be reckoned in making the determination, namely the loss through replacement of a vocabulary item. The fact that the loss might be due to simple substitution, to change in meaning, or to phonological change to the point of nonrecognition was held to be of no significance in making the calculations.

To use the method to show rate of change, it was necessary to assume (on the basis of calculations in regard to certain documented language families) that replacement of the selected basic vocabulary items proceeded at a relatively steady rate, roughly around 20% per millennium. There has been much criticism of the procedure and some say flatly that the method is unreliable. In the hands of intuitively gifted people, however, it has sometimes been a useful tool in detecting relationships not previously suspected and in providing, in some cases, an index of degree of closeness of relationship.

For the most part, those who have derived a certain amount of satisfaction from their use of some kind of lexicostatistical methods have been those who have been exceedingly careful to base their calculations on true cognates backed by sound comparative method.

[5] A good description of the method is found in Dell H. Hymes, "Lexicostatistics so far", *Current Anthropology*, 1(1), 3-44 (1960).

## 4.23 *The reconstruction method*

The reconstruction method is the comparative method carried through to the point of making as many actual reconstructions as possible. It is still the most reliable as well as the most rigorous method. However, it cannot be used when quick results are expected. Indeed the very fact that it requires so much time and labor has meant that it has been used far less widely than it should be.

It should also be emphasized that the reconstruction method is the most reliable method of validating not only close relationships but more remote relationships as well. Some people are impatient with this and feel that progress can only be made by setting up what are often called 'phyla' (large language groupings) by other methods, often highly personal and intuitive. Some even feel that in cases of remote relationship the principle of sound correspondences cannot be used. This is an overstatement of the difficulties involved in working out deeper relationships. It is much more likely to be true that some remote relationships are recoverable only in this way.

### 4.3 THE NEED FOR A LINGUISTIC PREHISTORY OF NORTH AMERICA

Linguists and cultural anthropologists alike have tended to be so concerned about the problem of the genetic classification of the languages of North America that they have tended to overlook the potential of linguistic reconstruction as a tool for recovering great quantities of historical information of both the diffused and genetic types.[6] This leads us to ask, What have we a right to expect from

---

[6]   To the great detriment of the proper development of the historical linguistics of American Indian languages, the age-old problem of diffused vs. genetic became an outright either-or proposition. Diffusion was especially championed by those who were dubious of proposed deep-seated genetic connections. Consequently, the importance of the proper study of borrowed words and other types of diffused material in the unravelling of historical sequences is rarely mentioned in the literature on North American Indian languages. The valuable lesson taught by the well-known cognation of German *strasse*: Eng. *street*, even though ultimately descended from an old borrowing from Latin (*via*) *strāta*, has

the comparative or reconstruction method and what will we have to do to fulfill these expectations?

First of all, it cannot be too vigorously maintained that the chief value of the comparative method does NOT lie in its utility for confirming relationships. Confirmation is merely a by-product. The really important thing about the use of the comparative method is that it provides us a means whereby we can reconstruct protolanguages by comparing sister languages and thus, when the job is fully done, obtain a comparative grammar and dictionary of each protolanguage. But notwithstanding the fact that we have the necessary methods at our disposal, we do not yet have a full comparative grammar and dictionary[7] of any American Indian protolanguage. When we have as many of these as we have linguistic families to work on (I am here speaking of those of relatively shallow time depths), we shall have a truly tremendous amount of information about the linguistic situation in North America as it

---

never been made use of in American Indian studies for the good and sufficient reason that the reconstruction of protolanguages of shallow time depth is as important for the detection of old loanwords at that level as it is for the detection of deeper genetic connections. The truth of the matter is that both cognates AND borrowed words have a story to tell about earlier connections.

[7]   The nearest thing we have to a comparative grammar is Bloomfield's excellent sketch "Algonquian", but it covers only four Central languages and these not in their entirety. A full comparative grammar will need to encompass as many other Algonkian languages as possible, not only others of the Central type (such as Shawnee and Miami-Peoria-Illinois) but also those of the East (especially Delaware, Micmac and Penobscot or closely related dialect) and those of the West (Arapaho, Cheyenne, and Blackfoot). Hockett's admirable beginning of a comparative dictionary ("Central Algonquian vocabulary...") suffers from exactly the same limitations and consequently even in the material already published there are likely to be many omissions as far as the actual prototypical vocabulary is concerned, gaps which can some day be filled when other Algonkian languages are brought into the picture. For example, a vocabulary item attested only in one of Hockett's chosen Central languages will not appear in his dictionary even though it may appear in every other Algonkian language on which we have information. Sapir spent many years of his life working on the comparative grammar and vocabulary of Athapaskan but did not succeed in satisfying himself that any part of it was ready to be published. Harry Hoijer has 'inherited' this material and has added much to it of his own. When it is ready for publication it will be much more comprehensive than the Algonkian material since no arbitrary limitation of the languages used has been imposed.

existed approximately three to five thousand years ago, that is, 1000-3000 B.C. By 'information about the linguistic situation', I mean rather precise information about the words and ideas expressed in these protolanguages and also the types of grammars they had. In other words, we would have information much like the linguistic information contained in the ancient written languages of Europe and Asia (e.g. Latin, Greek, Sanskrit, etc.). In recent years linguists have looked for short cuts in determining relationships that may extend back ten thousand or so years ago but have often neglected the more modest (but potentially much richer) goal of finding out as much as possible about the situation existing three to five thousand years ago.

By far the most distressing aspect of this rather obvious fact is that such information is still lacking even though it could be acquired by existing methods. That we still lack such potentially valuable information seems to be due to two factors, (1) lack of sufficient motivation to keep at the job over a long period of time, and (2) lack of sufficient trained manpower.

The achievement of the goal I have in mind would require the labors of scores of trained scholars. For example, to put it in round numbers, we need 5-10 people working steadily on the comparison of each linguistic family; in other words, 5-10 people working on comparative Algonkian, another 5-10 on comparative Athapaskan, and another 5-10 each on Uto-Aztecan, Tanoan, Iroquoian, Siouan, Muskogean, Caddoan, Salishan, Wakashan, Yuman, Pomoan, Mayan, Mixtecan, and so on until the list is exhausted.[8] If we could once achieve a good knowledge of the various protolanguages that were in use around 2000-5000 years ago, we would then be in a

---

[8] There has been a gratifying upsurge of interest in comparative and other Algonkian studies in recent years (as recently as the last decade) and there are now almost the proposed number of people doing some kind of work on comparative Algonkian problems. None, however, are working 'steadily' in this field and many are doing work on other North American families as well. Uto-Aztecan has also been receiving increased attention lately, though the optimum number of people working has not been reached nor are any of them working 'steadily' on comparative problems within this one family. Of the other language families mentioned most are blessed with no more than one, or at most two, definitely part-time workers.

proper position to determine whether or not the application of the comparative method to these protolanguages can carry us back another two to five millennia.

Some of us have jumped the gun and made preliminary attempts at the comparison of two or more protolanguages (see 2.423)[9] but our efforts are hampered by the lack of full comparative dictionaries and by the lack of important information about diffusion and/or relationship that could be obtained from other protolanguages not yet reconstructed. All this remains for the future and its accomplishment will be as rewarding and as exciting as would be the discovery of an assemblage of written documents of previously unknown languages of 2000-4000 B.C.

[9] See also Robert E. Longacre, *Proto-Mixtecan* (=*Indiana University PRCAFL*, Publication 5) (Bloomington, Indiana, 1957); *id.*, "Amplification of Gudschinsky's Proto-Popolocan-Mixtecan", *IJAL*, 28.227-42 (1962); Sarah C. Gudschinsky, *Proto-Popotecan* (= *Indiana University Publ. in Anthropology and Linguistics*, Memoir 15) (Baltimore, 1959).

# 5. PREHISTORY AND DIFFUSION

## 5.1 LEXICAL BORROWING

In previous chapters emphasis has been placed on the reconstruction of protolanguages as a part of the general problem of genetic relationship. But genetic prehistory is not the only kind of linguistic prehistory. In terms of the overall prehistory of unwritten languages, it is as rewarding to uncover evidence of earlier contact as it is to find evidence of genetic relationship. It should be clear that if languages A and B are now widely separated, the uncovering of evidence of lexical borrowing from A to B or B to A indicates (1) that the two languages were once in contact or (2) that the diffusion has taken place through the medium of an intermediary language or languages. Sometimes the path may be difficult to trace, but at other times it is clear enough. For example, Abnaki, an Algonkian language of the northeastern area, was first written down by Father Rasles, a French missionary, in the late seventeenth century. His records make it clear, however, that these Indians had already been in contact with English because their word for 'hog', an imported animal, was *piks* (<Eng. 'pigs'), generalized by them as a singular.[1]

While it is relatively easy to determine the donor language when this is a European language, the problem becomes more difficult if both the donor language (DL) and the recipient language (RL) are

---

[1] They formed the plural through the use of their own animate plural suffix giving *piksak* 'hogs'. See Father Sebastian Rasles, *A dictionary of the Abnaki language* (= *Memoirs, American Academy of Arts and Sciences*, 1.370-574) (1833).

aboriginal. However, a few general guidelines can be laid out. (1) The phonological evidence must be taken into account. (If the presumed loan has *l* in A and *n* in B, the DL is A if A has both *l* and *n* and B has only *n* in their respective phonemic inventories). (2) The morphological evidence must be taken into account. (If the word has an etymology in A but not in B, then A is the DL.) (3) If both A and B have several congeners, the DL is likely to be the one whose congeners also have the term. (But if the term is widely used in both families, then the DL may be a third language, or the borrowing may even have taken place between the proto-languages; in this case the true origin may be difficult to determine). (4) If A has congeners and B has none, A is likely to be the DL if the term is widespread in the family, particularly if the regular sound correspondences which should pertain in the circumstances actually do pertain.

Contact prehistory, then, is of considerable interest and importance, even though it can be approached only through the careful study of loanwords and other diffused phenomena. Moreover, studies of language contact have received renewed attention in recent years[2] and it appears likely that more effort will be expended in this direction in the future. Unfortunately, studies of loanwords from one American Indian language to another are extremely rare.[3] There are several factors which have contributed to the neglect of such potentially valuable material. Among these are: (1) the lack of good grammars and dictionaries of adjacent languages in sufficient density for any given area, (2) a tendency to consider a loanword as somehow less respectable than a cognate, and (3) a disposition to discount the possibility of borrowing in certain semantic domains.

---

[2]  E.g., Uriel Weinreich, *Languages in contact* (New York, 1953).
[3]  Studies of linguistic borrowing in American Indian languages are almost invariably devoted to their adoption of words from European languages. Important as such studies are, they throw little light on intertribal contacts except insofar as European loanwords can be shown to have reached language A through contact with language B (in turn, possibly through language C, etc.) and not directly through contact with European speakers. But even this is rarely attempted.

One sometimes encounters the statement that we arc well- if not over-supplied with data on various languages of North America and that now all we need is to make proper use of what is already available. But the student who is seriously interested in the study of intertribal loanwords cannot accept this for a moment. All too often he finds that there are four or five grammatical sketches, a half dozen bodies of texts, and one or possibly two reasonably adequate dictionaries for an area in which perhaps thirty or forty languages were spoken. But a truly adequate study of the intertribal loans in such an area cannot be undertaken without full data on most if not all of the languages.

Problems of remote genetic relationship are also handicapped by derogatory attitudes toward loanwords. Almost every proposal of a remote tie-up that has ever been made has been met with the counterassertion that whatever resemblances there may be are due to borrowing. Surely this is just as nonrigorous as to assume prima facie cognation. The habit would scarcely merit attention, however, if it were not for the fact that there is almost always the implication that borrowings are useless artifacts which must be weeded out and thenceforth ignored. But loanwords are as important in tracing historical contacts as cognates are in tracing historical origins.

As an almost inevitable corollary of this attitude of contempt for loanwords is the reluctance of some investigators to accept the fact of borrowing even in cases which seem to be incontrovertible. Such reluctance, interestingly enough, usually takes the form of some kind of categorical exclusion. For example, basic numerals, or basic kin terms, or pronouns are among those categories most often mentioned as being unlikely candidates for this (presumed) inferior status.

All such generalizations and rationalizations are sheer mythology based on insufficient evidence. Let us face the facts of history squarely and without presuppositions. Let us not lose sight of the fact that even if languages of a given area are not genetically related (or at least not indubitably so), they are still very likely to show certain similarities. These similarities demand an explanation and their study is as much a part of the linguistic history of the area as is the study of genetic relationship.

In North America, as elsewhere in the world, words of fairly wide provenience have frequently diffused with the spread of the item they name. The wide range in the West of similar terms for 'tobacco' is a case in point. Similar examples could be cited for borrowings in a variety of semantic domains. A borrowing may even intrude into an existing sequence, such as a numeral system. Thus the Cherokee (Iroquoian) word for 'seven', *kahlkwo·ki*, does not resemble anything in other Iroquoian languages but appears to be borrowed from the neighboring Creek (Muskogean) *kulapâ·kin* (< *kul-* 'two' + *apâ·kin* 'added on').[4]

When words for flora and fauna are borrowed, it can at least be suspected that the RL is a later arrival in the area than the DL. The Creek word *acína* 'cedar' is virtually identical with Cherokee *atsina*, but which is the DL and which the RL is not clear. Both may have gotten the term from an unknown language. Hitchiti (Muskogean) *acin-i* (-i, noun suffix) probably borrowed the term from Creek since Hitchiti has borrowed many words from Creek. Did Proto-Muskogean lack a word for 'cedar'? This cannot be answered with certainty. The remaining Muskogean languages have a term *čuwahla* (Choctaw, Alabama, and Koasati) which may reflect the prototype. This word has in turn been borrowed into Biloxi (a Siouan language) as *tcuwa'hạna'* /*čuwahna*/.[5] It is clear that the isoglosses of the words for 'cedar' do not follow genetic boundaries in the Southeast. This is fairly typical of the problems regarding terms for many flora and fauna of the area.

But some words are so widespread in a given area that it is impossible to pinpoint the original DL. Among the aboriginal languages of the Southeast, for example, phonologically similar words for 'buffalo' are found throughout most of the area. There is Tunica *yániši*, Natchez *yanasah*, Cherokee *yahnsạ*, as well as the

---

[4] Floyd G. Lounsbury, "Iroquois-Cherokee linguistic relations", 15, and Mary R. Haas, "Comment on [Lounsbury]", 22, in *Symposium on Cherokee-Iroquois Culture* (= *Bureau of American Ethnology*, Bulletin 180) (Washington, 1961).
[5] The direction of borrowing is certain. The Muskogean languages have both *l* and *n* as phonemes, but Biloxi has only *n*.

similar terms in the several Muskogean languages, e.g. Choctaw *yaniš*, Alabama-Koasati *yanasa*; Hitchiti *yanas-i*, Creek *yanása*. The original DL is unknown and may very well be some language other than those cited.

Sometimes widespread similarities are probably to be attributed to onomatopoeia. But some resemblances are remarkably precise even if one allows for onomatopoeia. Words for 'goose' from the Southeast to California are a case in point. In the Southeast we have Natchez *la·lak*, Tunica *lálahki*. In California we have Yana (Hokan) *la·laki*, Mutsun (Costanoan) *lalak*, and Nisenan (Maiduan) *la·lak'* as well as the only slightly less similar Chimariko (Hokan) *lalo*, Pomoan (Hokan) *lala*, Luiseño (Uto-Aztecan) *laʔla*, and Southern Sierra Miwok (Miwokan) *laŋlaŋ*. Many other bird names show equally uneven but widespread distribution. They deserve further study.

Calques (or translation-loans) are also common among American aboriginal languages. Here it is somewhat more difficult to rule out independent invention, at least in noncontiguous areas. But sometimes the evidence is quite persuasive. Kato, an Athapaskan language of northern California, is the only Athapaskan language known to use as its word for 'four' a repetition of 'two', namely *nąkkaʔnąkkaʔ* 'four' (*nąkkaʔ* 'two'). All other Athapaskan languages, even those which are extremely close to Kato, both genetically and geographically, have separate words for 'four'. But Takelma, a Penutian language of southern Oregon, uses the same method as Kato for expressing 'four': *gamgam* 'four' (*gāʔm* 'two'). Did Kato borrow this device from Takelma? This is not certain, but no one doubts that the Athapaskans came into northern California from the north and it is conceivable that they were once in contact with the Takelma.

5.2 STRUCTURAL DIFFUSION

5.21 *The concept of the diffusion area*

Even among genetically unrelated languages striking structural resemblances are often found spread over wide geographical areas. These may encompass phonological resemblances (5.22), morpho-logico-syntactic resemblances, or semantic resemblances of various types, including classificatory schemes (5.23). Even more interesting is the fact that some rather specific resemblances may also occur in widely separated areas. In searching for an answer to the problem posed by such cases, three alternatives present themselves: (1) The resemblance is a clue to genetic relationship at a deep level, (2) it is a clue to earlier contact other than genetic, or (3) it is fortui-tous. Among the languages of North America, unfortunately, there has been a tendency to argue in favor of either (1) or (3). Very little consideration has been given to possibility (2).

Emeneau's concept of a linguistic area[6] is based on well-attested examples of structural diffusion across genetic boundaries. Others have argued for the use of other terms, such as 'convergence area',[7] but the phenomenon is the same. The term 'convergence', however, is not a happy one since it is normally used by anthropologists to refer to "the *independent apparently accidental* development of similarities between separate cultures"[8] whereas what is wanted is a term which would imply the development of similarities *through contact*. A much better term would be 'diffusion area',[9] which could then be used for culture areas[10] as well as linguistic areas and which could, moreover, be modified at will ('phonological diffusion area', etc.) for greater specificity.

At a time when others were trying drastically to reduce the number of genetic stocks in North America,[11] Boas was much

---

[6]   Murray B. Emeneau, "India as a Linguistic Area", *Lg.*, 32.3-16 (1956).
[7]   Uriel Weinreich, "On the compatibility of genetic relationship and conver-gent development", *Word*, 14.374-379 (1958). Reference is to p. 379.
[8]   *Webster's Third New International Dictionary*, unabridged. Emphasis added.
[9]   Emeneau has also suggested the term 'diffusion area' as being preferable to 'convergence area', but his primary preference is 'linguistic area', his original term. See Murray B. Emeneau, *India and Historical Grammar*, 27 (Annama-lainagar, 1965).
[10]   The term is an old one in anthropology. See, i.a., A. L. Kroeber, *Cultural and natural areas of native North America* (Berkeley and Los Angeles, 1939).
[11]   E.g., Paul Radin, "The genetic relationship of the North American Indian

disturbed by the clear existence of such diffusion areas among American Indian languages and was led to take an extreme position in regard to the problems of genetic relationship.[12]

> If the view expressed here is correct, then it is not possible to group American languages rigidly in a genealogical scheme in which each linguistic family is shown to have developed to modern forms, but we have to recognize that many of the languages have multiple roots. (p. 7)

This of course is a version of the *Mischsprache* theory and his remarks led him into sharp controversy with some of his most eminent students, Sapir and Kroeber among them. But one does not need to accept all the implications of the *Mischsprache* theory to recognize that the problems that were disturbing to Boas were genuine problems. Moreover, they are mostly problems of HIS-TORICAL[13] significance and should be viewed in that light. Some of these are illustrated in the following sections.


### 5.22 *Phonological diffusion*

The Pacific Coast area has long been known as a place of wide-spread phonological diffusion.[14] It is noted for complex consonantal systems, including glottalized consonants (not only stops but frequently spirants and sonorants as well), lateral spirants and affricates, back velar consonants and labio-velar consonants.

---

languages", *UCPAAE*, 14 (5). 489-502 (1919) and Edward Sapir, "Central and North American Indian languages", in *Encyclopaedia Britannica*[14], 5.128-141 (1929).

[12] Franz Boas, "Classification of American Indian languages", *Lg.*, 5.1-7 (1929).

[13] Boas also considered some resemblances, especially those traits distributed unevenly on a world-wide basis, to be "due to psychological causes", "The classification of American languages", *American Anthropologist*, 22.367-376 (1920).

[14] See especially Melville Jacobs, "The areal spread of sound features in the languages north of California", pp. 46-56, in *Papers from the Symposium on American Indian Linguistics* (= *UCPL*, 10.1-68) (Berkeley and Los Angeles, 1954).

Various combinations of these traits are found to persist across genetic boundaries again and again.

Tables XVI[15] and XVII[16] show the systems of thirteen languages (omitting Miami in Table XVII which is from another area) whose geographical range is from Alaska to Central California. At least eight linguistic families are represented: Athapaskan, Nadene (but including Athapaskan if Tlingit is actually related), Penutian, Salishan, Wakashan, Chemakuan, Ritwan (Yurok and Wiyot), and Hokan.

Moving from north to south the languages are Kutchin, Tlingit, Tsimshian, Bella Coola, Kwakiutl, and Quileute in Table XVI; then Tolowa, Yurok, and Wiyot with Karok and Shasta to the east of Yurok in Table XVII; finally, Klamath to the east of Shasta and Kashaya to the south again in Table XVI. The most striking features of the area are set off in boxes with solid lines. The following have been marked in this way: (1) Labio-velars (*kw* and/or *qw*, etc.)

---

[15] Plain stops and affricates *p, t, k, č*, etc. are voiceless unaspirated and *h* is added to show aspiration. The apostrophe is added to show glottalization of all stops and affricates as well as spirants and sonorants. The sources for the consonantal systems shown in Table XVI are as follows: Edward Sapir, Unpublished Kutchin materials; Constance Mary Naish, *A syntactic study of Tlingit* (unpublished doctoral dissertation, 1966) and Gillian Lorraine Story, *A morphological study of Tlingit* (unpublished doctoral dissertation, 1966); Franz Boas, "Tsimshian", pp. 283-422, in *Handbook of American Indian Languages*, Part I (= *Bureau of American Ethnology*, Bulletin 40, Part I) (Washington, 1911); Stanley Newman, "Bella Coola, I: Phonology", *IJAL*, 13.129-34 (1947); Franz Boas, "Kwakiutl", pp. 423-557, in *Handbook of American Indian Languages*, Part I; Manuel J. Andrade, "Quileute", pp. 149-292, in *Handbook of American Indian Languages*, Part 3 (Glückstadt-Hamburg-New York, 1933-38); M. A. R. Barker, *Klamath Grammar* (= *UCPL*, 32) (Berkeley and Los Angeles, 1964); Robert L. Oswalt, *Kashaya Texts* (= *UCPL*, 36) (Berkeley and Los Angeles, 1966).

[16] The sources for the consonantal systems in Table XVII are: Jane O. Bright, "The phonology of Smith River Athapaskan (Tolowa)", *IJAL*, 30.101-107 (1967); R. H. Robins, *The Yurok Language* (= *UCPL*, 15) (Berkeley and Los Angeles, 1958); Karl V. Teeter, *The Wiyot Language* (= *UCPL*, 37) (Berkeley and Los Angeles, 1964); William Bright, *The Karok Language* (= *UCPL*, 13) (Berkeley and Los Angeles, 1957); Shirley Silver, *The Shasta Language* (unpublished doctoral dissertation, 1966); C. F. Voegelin, *Shawnee Stems and the Jacob P. Dunn Miami Dictionary* (Indianapolis, 1937-40).

## Consonant systems of the Pacific Coast area

### KUTCHIN (Athapaskan)

```
?        h

                 qw  qwh q'w xw  x'w
                 q   qh  q'  x   x'
kw kwh  k'w xw  γw
k  k    k'  x   γ
ç  çh   ç'  ṣ̌  ẓ̌
č  čh   č'            nč
cy cyh  c'y sy  zy
c  ch   c'  s   z
tθ tθh  t'θ θ   δ
λ  λh   λ'  ł   l
t  th   t'           n   nt
             v  (m)
```

### TLINGIT (Nadene)

```
?        h

        qw  qwh q'w xw  x'w
        q   qh  q'  x   x'
        kw  kwh k'w xw  x'w
        k   kh  k'  x   x'  y
        č   čh  č'  š
        c   ch  c'  s   s'
        λ   λh  λ'  ł   l'
        t   th  t'           n
                     w
```

### TSIMSHIAN (Penutian?)

```
?        h

q  qh   q'  x̣
k  kh   k'  γ
ky kyh  k'y     y   y'
c  ch   c'  s
            ł   l   l'
t  th   t'          n   n'
p  ph   p'      w   w'  m   m'
```

### BELLA COOLA (Salish)

```
?        (h)

qw  q'w xw
q   q'  x̣
kw  k'w xw
k   k'  x
                y   y'
c   c'  s
    λ'  ł   l   l'
t   t'          n   n'
p   p'      w   w'  m   m'
```

## Table XVI (continued)

### KWAKIUTL (Wakashan)

ʔ     h,ḥ

| qw | qwh | q'w | x̣w |    |    |
|----|-----|-----|-----|----|----|
| q  | qh  | q'  | x̣  |    |    |
| kw | kwh | k'w | xw  |    |    |
| ky | kyh | k'y | xy  | y  | y' |
| c  | ch  | c'  | s   |    |    |
| ƛ  | ƛh  | ƛ'  | ł   | l  | l' |
| t  | th  | t'  |     | n  | n' |
| p  | ph  | p'  | w   | w' | m  | m' |

### QUILEUTE (Chemakuan)

ʔ     h

| qw | q'w | x̣w |   |
|----|-----|-----|---|
| q  | q'  | x̣  |   |
| kw | k'w | xw  |   |
| k  | k'  | x   |   |
| č  | č'  | š   | y |
| c  | c'  | s   |   |
| ƛ  | ƛ'  | ł   | l |
| t  | t'  | d   |   |
| p  | p'  | w   | b |

### KLAMATH (Penutian)

ʔ     h

| q | qh | q' |   |    |    |    |
|---|----|----|---|----|----|----|
| k | kh | k' |   |    |    |    |
| č | čh | č' | y | y' |    |    |
|   |    | s  |   |    |    |    |
|   |    | l  | l'|    |    |    |
| t | th | t' |   |    | n  | n' |
| p | ph | p' | w | w' | m  | m' |

### KASHAYA (Pomoan [Hokan])

ʔ     h

| q | qh | q' |   |   |    |   |
|---|----|----|---|---|----|---|
| k | kh | k' |   |   |    |   |
| ṭ | ṭh | ṭ' |   |   |    |   |
| č | čh | č' | š | y |    |   |
|   |    | c' | s |   |    |   |
|   |    |    | l |   |    |   |
| t | th | t' |   |   | n  | d |
| p | ph | p' | w |   | m  | b |

## TABLE XVII

*Yurok and Wiyot consonant systems compared with neighboring California languages and with Algonkian (Miami)*

| TOLOWA (Athapaskan) | YUROK | WIYOT |
|---|---|---|
| <pre>ʔ    h<br>kw  k'w xw<br>k   k'  x  ɣ<br>        č'  ş<br>č čh č' š  y<br>  ch    s<br>        ł  l<br>t th t'      n  n'<br>p         w m  m'</pre> | <pre>ʔ    h<br>kw  k'w<br>k   k'     ɣ<br>č   č' (š) y<br>           s<br>        ł  l<br>t   t'     r  n<br>p   p'     w  m</pre> | <pre>(ʔ)  h<br>kw kwh<br>k  kh  ɣ<br>č  čh š    y<br>c  ch s<br>       ł  l<br>t  th  ɽ r n<br>p  ph  β w m</pre> |

| KAROK (Hokan) | SHASTA (Hokan) | MIAMI (Algonkian) |
|---|---|---|
| <pre>ʔ h<br>k x<br>č   y<br>    s<br>t θ r n<br>p f v m</pre> | <pre>ʔ    h<br>k  k'  x<br>č  č'    y<br>c  c'  s<br>t  t'    r n<br>p  p'    w m</pre> | <pre>(ʔ) h<br>k<br>č š y<br>    s<br>t  l n<br>p  w m</pre> |

in Kutchin, Tlingit, Bella Coola, Kwakiutl, Quileute, Tolowa, Yurok, and Wiyot; (2) back velars ($q$, etc.) in Tlingit, Tsimshian, Bella Coola, Kwakiutl, Quileute, Klamath, and Kashaya; (3) glottalized stops in Kutchin, Tlingit, Tsimshian, Bella Coola, Kwakiutl, Quileute, Tolowa, Yurok, Shasta, and Klamath; (4) glottalized spirants in Tlingit; (5) glottalized sonorants in Tsimshian, Bella Coola, Kwakiutl, and Klamath; (6) lateral affricates and spirants in Kutchin, Tlingit, Bella Coola, Kwakiutl, and Quileute plus lateral spirants only ($l$ and/or $l$') in Tsimshian, Tolowa, Yurok, and Wiyot.

In addition a three-way contrast in the stop series (unaspirated, aspirated, and glottalized) is shown by braces and occurs in Kutchin, Tlingit, Tsimshian, Kwakiutl, Tolowa, Klamath, and Kashaya. Most other languages have a two-way contrast, usually plain and glottalized, as in Bella Coola, Quileute, Yurok, and Shasta, but occasionally plain and aspirated, as in Wiyot. Karok is very untypical of the languages in the area in having only one series of stops.

There are also interesting negative traits in parts of the area. Shown is the extreme paucity of labials in Kutchin, Tlingit, and Tolowa. Quileute is notable in lacking nasals (since $b$ and $d$ have replaced $m$ and $n$ of its nearest relative, Chemakum, not shown in the tables). Absence of nasals is also a feature of Nitinat (a Wakashan language not shown) which has not only $b$ and $d$ in place of Nootka (not shown) $m$ and $n$ but also $b$' and $d$' in place of Nootka $m$' and $n$'. A similar lack of nasals is also a feature of some Salish languages, e.g. Snohomish.[17]

Yurok and Wiyot (Table XVII), languages of northern California, share some of the special traits of the Pacific Coast area with their immediate neighbors in marked contrast to the Algonkian languages (of which Miami has been taken as an example) with which they are genetically most nearly allied. Yurok has glottalized consonants, Wiyot has aspirated consonants, and both have the lateral spirant ($l$). There is also a small subarea here in which $r$ is a common consonant.

[17] Thomas M. Hess, "Snohomish chameleon morphology", *IJAL*, 32.350-356 (1966).

Tables XVI and XVII show that languages spoken in contiguous areas can come to share a number of phonological traits without regard for genetic boundaries. But suppose two languages which are geographically far apart and not known to be genetically related turn out to have strong phonological resemblances. Can we assume earlier contact between them, i.e., that they were once part of the same phonological diffusion area? This is a difficult question. However, the possibility of historical connection (genetic and/or contact) should not be ruled out entirely. An especially interesting case is that of Yuchi, a language isolate of the Southeast. It was surrounded by Creek (Muskogean), Cherokee (Iroquoian), Catawba (divergent Siouan), and two other languages (Cusabo and Yamasee) which are not definitely classified because of early extinction.

|  | Cherokee |  | Catawba |
|---|---|---|---|
| Creek |  | YUCHI | Cusabo |
|  | Yamasee |  |  |

Yuchi has several rather specialized phonological traits, among them glottalized stops, spirants, and semivowels. Except for the presence of a bilabial *f*, a marked Muskogean trait, and the lateral spirant *l* (also in Muskogean and some Cherokee dialects), it does not bear much resemblance to its known recent neighbors. But when we compare it with Dakota (a group of Siouan dialects of the Plains), we find several quite striking resemblances. It has been suggested that Yuchi is a distant relative of the Siouan languages[18] and so the resemblance may possibly be due in some measure to this fact (if true). But this does not rule out much more recent *contact* (quite apart from possible relationship) with Siouan languages, e.g. Ofo and perhaps others now extinct. The phonological resemblance of Yuchi to Dakota and Ofo as well as the considerable lack of resemblance to Creek and Cherokee is shown in Table XVIII.[19]

[18] Edward Sapir, "Central and North American Indian languages".
[19] Sources for Yuchi, Creek and Cherokee consonant systems are my own unpublished field notes. Yuchi is also found in Günter Wagner, "Yuchi", pp. 293-383, in *Handbook of American Indian Languages*, Part 3, but some features, such as *y'* and *w'*, are missing there. Dakota is taken from Franz Boas

TABLE XVIII

*The Yuchi consonant system compared to Siouan Languages and to neighboring languages of the Southeast*

|  | YUCHI |  |  |  |  |  |  | DAKOTA (Siouan) |  |  |  |  |  |  |
|---|---|---|---|---|---|---|---|---|---|---|---|---|---|---|
| ʔ | h |  |  |  |  |  |  | ʔ | h |  |  |  |  |  |
| k | kh | kʼ | x |  |  |  |  | k | kh | kʼ | x | xʼ | γ |  |
| č | čh | čʼ | š | šʼ | y | yʼ |  | č | čh | čʼ | š | šʼ | ž | y |
| c | ch | cʼ | s | sʼ |  |  |  |  |  | s | sʼ | z |  |  |
| t | th | tʼ |  |  |  | n | nʼ | t | th | tʼ |  |  | n |  |
|  |  | ł | łʼ | l | lʼ |  |  |  |  |  | l |  |  |  |
| p | ph | pʼ | f | fʼ | w | wʼ | m mʼ | p | ph | pʼ |  | w | m |  |

| OFO (Siouan) |  |  |  |  |  |  | CREEK (Muskogean) |  |  |  | CHEROKEE (Iroquoian) |  |  |  |
|---|---|---|---|---|---|---|---|---|---|---|---|---|---|---|
|  | h |  |  |  |  |  |  | h |  |  | ʔ | h |  |  |
| k | kh |  |  |  |  |  | k |  |  |  | k | kh |  |  |
| č | čh | (š) | y |  |  |  | č | y |  |  | č | čh | y hy |  |
|  | s | sh |  |  |  |  | s |  |  |  | s |  |  |  |
| t | th |  | n |  |  |  | t | n |  |  | t | th | n hn |  |
|  | l |  |  |  |  |  | ł | l |  |  | λ | λh | l hl[ł] |  |
| b p | ph | f | fh | w | m |  | p f | w | m |  |  |  | w hw (m) |  |

The glottalized series of stops and spirants[20] shown in boxes and the three-way contrast of stops shown by braces are particular

and Ella Deloria, *Dakota Grammar* (= *Memoirs of the National Academy of Sciences*, vol. XXIII, Second Memoir) (Washington, 1941) and Ofo has been extracted from lexical items in James Owen Dorsey and John R. Swanton, *A dictionary of the Biloxi and Ofo languages* (= *Bureau of American Ethnology, Bulletin 47*) (Washington, 1912).

[20] The glottalized spirants in Dakota are clusters and they may also be clusters in Yuchi. We are here comparing phonetic traits, not phonemes.

traits shared by Yuchi and Dakota. The bilabial fricative [φ] is found in both Yuchi and Ofo and both may have been influenced by Muskogean. The fact that Proto-Siouan *x and *s have shifted to Ofo s and f, respectively, does not invalidate this possibility. The presence of a lateral spirant l in Yuchi may also be the result of Muskogean influence. The two-letter combinations in the Cherokee chart are clusters, but some are phonetic units, e.g. hl, which is pronounced [ł], perhaps also the result of Muskogean influence. Another (now extinct) dialect of Cherokee had hr [R] instead.

Gross phonological traits have historical significance not only as clues to genetic relationship (in regard to which phonology can be drastically altered as was illustrated in the Pacific Coast area) but perhaps more often as clues to recent or fairly recent contact. But best results in tracing contact possibilities cannot be obtained unless ALL of the languages of a given area are carefully plotted. Our records are all too often deficient in crucial data for such purposes. Nevertheless it would be worth while to chart the consonant systems of all of North America. If carefully done it should reveal (1) many features of recent phonological diffusion areas, and (2) the possible outlines of some of the earlier phonological diffusion areas.

### 5.23 Diffusion of classificatory schemes

Most languages of the world have one or more types of arbitrary classificatory schemes which reflect covert taxonomies of greater or less complexity. Most of these reflect a categorization of entities,[21] and the grammatical devices which reveal the classi-

---

[21] The study of these is all too often neglected not only in lesser known but in well-known languages as well. The three-way categorization implied in English by the intransitive-transitive pairs, lie-lay, sit-set, and stand-stand has not, to my knowledge, been worked out in detail. Observe the noninterchangeability of the noun objects in the following sentences: (1) Lay *the book* on the table. (2) Set *the kettle* on the stove. (3) Stand *the easel* by the window. The fact that there are neutral verbs like 'place', 'put' which can replace the positional verbs may mean that the categorization is becoming weaker, but it does not mean that it is lacking.

fication are of two main types, (1) those which are appended directly to the noun referring to the entity, and (2) those which are always referential, i.e. form a part of the agreement system. Sometimes the categorization is reflected in both these ways.

Generally speaking, there is a series of binary oppositions involved in these taxonomies[22] and the complexity depends on the manner in which these are combined. Typical oppositions are the following:

| Singular | : | plural |
|---|---|---|
| Individual | : | mass |
| Human | : | nonhuman |
| Animate | : | inanimate |
| Male | : | female |
| Vertical | : | horizontal |
| Rigid | : | flexible |
| Liquid | : | solid |

Sometimes a three-way contrast is involved, viz.

| Singular | : | dual | : | plural |
|---|---|---|---|---|
| Male | : | female | : | neuter |
| Vertical | : | squatting | : | horizontal |
| Liquid | : | viscuous | : | solid |

But it often happens that such two- and three-way oppositions are mixed together in unusual ways. Such mixing is found, for example, in the classificatory verb systems of the Athapaskan languages.[23] These languages have two sets of verbs whose use depends upon the classification of the noun referred to.[24] One is a set of neuter

[22] I owe this insight to a paper by Keith H. Basso, "The Western Apache classificatory verb system: A formal analysis" (1968).
[23] The Athapaskan languages have spread during the past 1500-2000 years into three main areas, (1) Alaska and western Canada, (2) the Pacific Coast as far south as northern California, and (3) the Southwest to beyond the Mexican border.
[24] For a description of the categories involved in several of these languages, see William Davidson, L. W. Elford, and Harry Hoijer, "Athapaskan classificatory verbs", in Harry Hoijer and Others, *Studies in the Athapaskan languages* (= *UCPL*, 29) (Berkeley and Los Angeles, 1963).

verbs the choice among which depends on the classification of the subject, thus, 'a living being lies', 'a round object lies', etc. The other is a set of active verbs the choice among which depends on the classification of the object, thus, 'to pick up a living being', 'to pick up a round object', etc. Mixing occurs in various ways, but some of it is quite consistent from language to language. In Table XIX[25] fourteen of the most usual kinds of categories are shown. To highlight their widespread use among the Athapaskan languages an indication of their presence or absence in one of the languages from each of the three main areas is marked in the table. A similar type of categorization is also found in other, nonrelated languages. Two striking examples are Takelma and Klamath, two not very closely related members of the Penutian stock. These languages have semantic classificatory schemes which bear a remarkable resemblance to those of some of their Athapaskan neighbors. Their geographical contiguity or near-contiguity to Athapaskan languages of the Pacific area is shown below.[26]

*Galice*

*Chasta Costa*      KLAMATH

TAKELMA

*Tolowa*      (Shasta)

(Yurok)      (Karok)

*Hupa*

(Wiyot)

*Mattole*

The possibility that the similarity in semantic categories among Takelma, Klamath and the Athapaskan languages is due to diffusion deserves careful consideration.

[25] Parentheses around a number in Table XIX show mixing. Thus (3) in row 6 means that 6 is expressed by the same verbs as 3. (The distinction is therefore semantic but not morphological). A repeated number, as 7,7 in row 7, means there are two separate but similar categories in the particular language. The device c/3 in row 12 means that category 12 is 'composed of' items classified as 3 in the singular.

[26] Takelma and Klamath are shown in small capital letters. The Athapaskan languages are shown in italized type. A few other non-Athapaskan and non-Penutian languages are shown in parentheses.

## TABLE XIX
### Classificatory schemes in Athapaskan languages and in other non-Athapaskan languages

| | CHIPEWYAN (Ath.) | NAVAHO (Ath.) | HUPA (Ath.) | TAKELMA (Pen.) | KLAMATH (Pen.) | CHEROKEE (Iroq.) | CREEK (Musk.) |
|---|---|---|---|---|---|---|---|
| 1. Living being | 1 | 1 | 1 | 1 | | 1 | |
| 2. Round object | 2 | 2 | 2 | 2 | 2 | 2 | |
| 3. Long rigid object | 3 | 3 | 3 | 3 | 3,3 | 3 | |
| 4. Broad flexible obj. (fabric) | 4 | 4 | 4 | 4 | 4,4 | 4 | (13) |
| 5. Long flexible obj. (rope) | 5 | 5 | 5 | 5 | | | |
| 6. Empty container | (3) | (8) | | 6 | 6 | | |
| 7. Container with contents | 7,7 | 7 | 7 | | 7 | 7 | |
| 8. Bundle or package | | 8 | | | | | |
| 9. Liquid | | * | | | | | (14) |
| 10. Grain, sand, hay | 10 | 10 | 10 | 10 | 10 | | |
| 11. Mud, dough | 11 | 11 | 11 | ** | 11 | | |
| 12. Aggregate or set | | c/3 | c/4 | | c/5 | | |
| 13. Dual | (5) | | (5) | (5) | | | 13 |
| 14. Plural | (5) | c/2 | | | | | 14 |

*Found in the closely related Western Apache, but not in Navaho.
**Categorized in the transitive, but not in the intransitive.

A more puzzling type of problem, however, exists on the other side of the continent. Cherokee, an Iroquoian language, has a classificatory system identical with the most common Athapaskan categories, viz. 1, 2, 3, 4, and 7 in Table XIX. No other Iroquoian language is known to have anything similar to this system. Was it diffused into Cherokee? If so, from what source? Was Cherokee somehow once part of a former diffusion area which also included some of the Athapaskan languages? Again, these questions deserve serious consideration, regardless of the ultimate answers.

One curious feature of all Athapaskan classificatory verb schemes is the mixing in of the category of number. Thus the same verb that is used with rope-like objects in the singular is also used to mark the dual and/or plural of objects of other shapes. Creek, a Muskogean language of the Southeast, contains the remnants (or the beginnings) of a similar system. The language has several sets of suppletive verbs, normally distinguished for three numbers, singular, dual, and plural. But side by side with this number categorization, there is a shape categorization in which a normally dual verb is always used with cloth-like objects (in any number) and a normally plural verb is always used with liquid entities. What is the origin of this mixed categorization? Is it through Cherokee influence? Or do we have here another possible example pointing to a former diffusion area of which both Cherokee and Creek formed a part?

There is another kind of semantic categorization that is much more commonly found in the Southeast. This is a categorization of position, namely, horizontal or lying, indifferent or sitting (squatting), and vertical or standing. It is often mixed with categories like animate vs. inanimate, human vs. nonhuman, male vs. female. It is found with greater or less elaboration in Tunica, Chitimacha, Biloxi (a Siouan language), and Yuchi. It is also reported for Winnebago, a Siouan language of the Midwest. In the related Dakota, however, it is found only in traces but the language appears also to contain traces of a classificatory system which resembles in a vague way the elaborate system of the Athapaskan languages.

The task of tracing out semantic diffusion areas has only just begun. Better studies of classificatory systems are urgently needed, but the possibilities are vast. Serious historical studies will benefit greatly if, along with the more vigorous application of the comparative method to genetic studies, we also begin to devise more rigorous and more effective ways of attacking the vast range of diffusion problems that have been almost completely ignored.

# AMERICAN INDIAN LANGUAGES
# AND HISTORICAL LINGUISTICS

1. Notwithstanding[1] important theoretical advances of the twentieth century, the fact remains that the development of the comparative method in the nineteenth century is the greatest triumph ever attained in the field of linguistics. The discovery of the relationship of the Indo-European languages, and, more important, the demonstration of the possibility of reconstructing actual proto-forms of words still in current use in the everyday languages of Europe and India, stimulated the minds of men in a way that is scarcely conceivable today. Comparative philology was widely acclaimed as the queen of the historical sciences, no less glorious than archaeology and geology which were at that time also inflicting on the world more discoveries than the world was ready for.

The great discoveries of Indo-European philology were based, as was no doubt inevitable, on the use of written materials. Having demonstrated the relationship of the languages of the Indo-European family, it was not long before scholars began to search for new worlds to conquer. Some turned their attention to other written languages, to Semitic, Egyptian, Turkish, and many others. But some scholars were not satisfied to stop here. Sooner or later the fact had to be faced up to that there were more unwritten than written languages in the world. What about the languages of Africa? of the Pacific? of the Americas? Here indeed were problems to test the mettle of even the most indefatiguable scholars.

2. I think it is reasonable to assert that the Americas have posed some of the most critical historical problems ever faced by linguists.

---

[1] This paper was read at the Third Conference on American Indian Languages held at the University of California, Los Angeles, in August, 1966.

APPENDIX: AMERICAN INDIAN LANGUAGES      99

Four centuries after Columbus, Max Müller, in the last revision of his famous lectures published in 1899, says:

The greatest diversity of opinion prevails with regard to the languages of America. Some scholars see nothing but diversity, others discover everywhere traces of uniformity, if not in the radical elements, at least in the formal structure of these languages. (p. 451)

Moreover, by that time it was not necessary to say anything even half so frustrating about any other area of the world.

A quarter of a century later (1924) Holger Pedersen is still forced to express a benumbed sort of bewilderment:

It is still uncertain into what large groups the American world of languages should be divided .... Much has been accomplished in the study of these languages, especially by Franz Boas and Edward Sapir, but even yet we have not got beyond a picture of dizzying complexity: more than one hundred and twenty different *families* of languages are computed. It is incredible that there should be no kinship at all among some of these; but a peculiar course of linguistic development may make it difficult to discover what the original relationships were. (p. 137)

In speaking of 120 different families, Pedersen was of course referring to both Americas, for the famous Powell classification into 58 families for North America north of Mexico had already appeared in 1891, with a reduction to 55 achieved by 1915.

There can be little doubt that from the beginning the one *overwhelming* fact about the languages of the Americas has been their diversity. And in the face of diversity there is after all only one reasonable thing to do and that is to classify. It has indeed been justly said that even a poor classification is better than no classification. But the diversity in the Americas is so great that even a poor classification has been hard to come by.

The grossest kind of linguistic classification is, of course, the geographical one.[2] As a general rule it is used solely as a labelling

[2]  In earlier times racial classification was also sometimes used, though combined with what was then known about genealogical classification. "[Friedrich] Müller and [Franz Nikolaus] Finck arrange the languages according to the different races of man, Müller distinguishing the languages of wooly-haired, smooth-haired, and curly-haired races. Finck begins where Müller stops: he classifies Caucasian, Mongolian, American, and Ethiopian races." (Pedersen, p. 101).

device, but quite aside from this accurate knowledge of the facts of linguistic geography, when properly used, *can* constitute a very important historical tool. But a geographical classification does not require the classifier to have any knowledge whatever of the content of the languages being classified. (It is not unknown for even nonexistent languages to be classified). When the actual content of the languages is known, or at least partially known, there are two ways in which they can be classified: (1) genealogically, and (2) typologically.

American Indian languages have served and continue to serve as a supreme test of both types of classification. Although the two types are often considered to be competitive or complementary, they are actually neither. All languages, written or unwritten, living or dead, are amenable to both types of classification provided a sufficient amount of their content is known. When we say that language X can be classified genealogically and language Y cannot, we only mean that language X has known relatives and language Y has none. Hence the genealogical classification of Y is as an orphan, or, in other words, a language isolate.

Another source of confusion about the two kinds of classification arises from the fact that related languages are likely to be typologically more similar than unrelated languages. We also have plenty of testimony to the fact that geographically contiguous languages may also have typological similarities. This is the pervasive fact that has led scholars to develop the idea of a "linguistic area".[3] But typological classification *par excellence* does not justify its existence on these bases. Although it has to be borne in mind that typological classification has not yet reached a high level of sophistication, the best typologists do have a clear goal in mind. It is to set up a typological matrix that will reveal similarities between languages even in cases where these cannot (at least presumptively) be attributed to genetic relationship or to geographical contiguity.

3. As was stated earlier, in the face of great diversity, the first thing to do is to arrive at some sort of classification. And for the

[3]  See M. B. Emeneau, "India as a Linguistic Area", *Lg.*, 32.3-16 (1956).

pursuance of the proper goals of historical linguistics, a genealogical classification has the most to offer since it provides a set of
working hypotheses about possible historical connections. At the
same time we are still far from having achieved a final genealogical
classificatory scheme for North America, nor indeed can this ever
be completed without reference to South America, the Pacific and
Asia. Consequently there will probably never be an end to new
classificatory schemes. Nor is this in itself deplorable. Scholars
cannot be scholars if they close their minds to new hypotheses. But
classificatory schemes tend to be overrated, and suggestions of
connections of great antiquity seem more glamorous than recent
ones. Cultural anthropologists, in particular, have demanded that
all languages be placed in one genealogical scheme or another. At
the same time they have failed to grasp the nature and extent of the
work that is required to set up a firm classification, and some of
them even express doubt about linguists' ability to *make* a classification, since linguists are so prone to disagree. Kroeber, in 1960, was
even ready to abandon "the comparative genetic technique" because
there is no evidence for its utility at great time depths:[4]

The century-and-a half old comparative genetic technique ... is a splendid
tool for confirming similarities within diversifications that have been
going on for some millennia — perhaps up to 5,000 years, perhaps to
7,000. But there comes a point in the past — perhaps 10,000 years ago,
perhaps less — at which the method no longer yields reliable results.
(p. 21)

Kroeber has completely failed to understand the nature of the
comparative method and what it can do. He and many other
cultural anthropologists are interested in the comparative method
*only* for its utility in demonstrating genetic relationship. This is the
grossest kind of underrating of what the comparative method can
do. Indeed it is time to educate cultural anthropologists and
possibly even some linguists to the fact that "the chief value of the
comparative method does *not* lie in its utility for confirming
relationships. Confirmation is merely a by-product."[5] But precisely

[4] A. L. Kroeber, "Statistics, Indo-European, and taxonomy", *Lg.*, 36.1-21
(1960).
[5] See p. 75 of the present volume.

because comparative linguistics is still the least developed phase of American Indian linguistic study, the method has so far proved very little beyond what had already been determined by the use of the inspection method. It is no wonder that its utility strikes the non-comparativist as limited.

Nevertheless, the comparative method is beyond any doubt the most important historical tool ever devised in linguistics. And in spite of earlier doubts about its feasibility for unwritten languages, it is in some ways even more valuable for these than for written languages for the very good reason that it gives us a great deal of the kind of material that is otherwise available only from ancient written records. And as far as the Americas are concerned we have scarcely begun to make use of it.

4.1 The comparative method enables us to reconstruct proto-languages. For a given protolanguage we need materials (grammars and dictionaries) on as many sister languages as are available. Even though good preliminary results can be obtained by choosing a sample of the sister languages, as has been demonstrated by Bloomfield and Dempwulff and others, full benefits cannot be attained without making use of all known sister languages. When working with unwritten languages the most satisfying results are obtained by comparing languages whose parent was spoken around 2000-3000 years ago. Moreover the labor required in such an endeavor is very great, though varying of course in proportion to the number of languages involved in the comparison. But once the job is properly done we have good knowledge of a parent language of an antiquity approximating that of Latin in relation to the modern Romance languages. Now Indo-Europeanists did not have to go through the labor of reconstructing Proto-Romance before they could continue their study of deeper relationships within Indo-European. They already had Latin, a written language of antiquity; they also had Greek, and later on Sanskrit, as well as other ancient languages. But for the American languages we have no such treasures, we have to reconstruct them. Indo-Europeanists were thus able to begin at a point we have not yet reached. And the work of reconstructing protolanguages, being extremely painstaking (and requiring much descriptive work beforehand, if this has not already been done), has not gone forward the way it should have in large part because it has received very little encouragement from any quarter. Perhaps the strongest deterrent has come from within linguistics itself. It is ironical that Bloomfield, who provided in his Proto-Algonkian work the most elegant example available of what it means to reconstruct a protolanguage (even though he did not finish the task), was also the one who laid the foundations for a school of descriptive linguistics which shortly became imbued with a strong *ahistorical* bias.[6] Descriptive linguistics and historical linguistics came to be treated as if they were poles apart. To be sure, the trend did not start with Bloomfield; it had already gained considerable momentum in Europe (de Saussure) and America (Boas) some time before. Indeed Sapir, another excellent comparativist in American Indian languages (noted especially for his work on Uto-Aztecan and Athapaskan) was already complaining of the lack of interest in comparative matters in 1917:[7]

... the Bureau has not yet fairly reached the comparative stage of linguistic work, but is still, and for quite some time to come necessarily will be, mainly concerned with descriptive labors. Nevertheless, I do not believe that *this almost total lack of emphasis on comparative work* is altogether due to the fact that so much remains to be done in the amassing of lexical and text materials.... *Comparative work in linguistics*, if it is to be of any scientific value, *requires a keenly sensitive historical consciousness in the handling of linguistic phenomena.* It is precisely the historical interpretation of cultural elements, however, that has up to the recent past been most conspicuously absent in Americanistic work. The lack of linguistic studies of a comparative nature is merely a symptom of this general defect. (p. 81) [Emphasis mine.]

---

[6] Ahistoricism — the scrupulous avoidance of allowing one's knowledge of the history of a language to influence one in any way in one's analysis and description of a language — was carried to extremes. In some instances, it became what might even be called "counter-historicism". If two kinds of solution to a problem seemed possible, the one known NOT to be historically accurate was all too often perversely preferred.

[7] Edward Sapir, "Linguistic publications of the Bureau of American Ethnology, a general review", *IJAL*, 1.76-81 (1917).

But thirty-five years later we were even worse off. At the peak of post-Bloomfieldian ahistoricism, Voegelin and Harris[8] comment on Sapir's remarks in the following negative terms:

Sapir's plea for the training of anthropologists in comparative linguistics must have been applauded by all who heard it in classical and modern language departments, where sound linguistics was equated to comparative linguistics. The same reaction, however, could scarcely have been expected in American anthropology, because comparative linguistic work, strictly speaking, was rarely attempted in anthropology … .

… To be regarded as linguistically strong during the two decades from 1913 to 1933 [the date of the publication of Bloomfield's *Language*] a linguist had to know comparative linguistics — which generally meant training in Indo-European languages — whether or not he intended to pursue comparative work in one or another American Indian language family … . Besides Athapaskan, comparative work was done in Uto-Aztecan and particularly and most rigorously in the Algonquian family. But such comparative linguistic work as was actually done in these decades attracted little attention in anthropology; reports of much of the comparative work then carried on still remain in manuscript form (pp. 323-324).

The time was not propitious for striking out in favor of increasing the knowledge and appreciation of comparative linguistics among anthropologists.

4.2 But the irony associated with Bloomfield's work was not the only irony. Sapir, by constructing a comprehensive classificatory system composed of six divisions (published in 1929)[9] also unintentionally contributed to the decline of comparative linguistics. He gave the anthropologists the neat scheme they apparently wanted — one which had no loose ends — and, in place of the "dizzying complexity" seen by Pedersen, simplicity appeared to rule. Worse yet, Sapir's name was so closely associated with comparative linguistics, it was even largely taken for granted that he must have accomplished this miracle through the rigorous application of the

---

[8]   C. F. Voegelin and Z. S. Harris, "Training in anthropological linguistics", *American Anthropologist*, 54.322-327 (1952).
[9]   Edward Sapir, "Central and North American Indian languages", *Encyclopaedia Britannica*[14], 5.128-41 (1929). Reprinted in *Selected Writings of Edward Sapir*, ed. David G. Mandelbaum 167-78 (Berkeley-Los Angeles, 1949).

comparative method.[10] And before long Sapir's scheme (even though described by himself as "far from demonstrable in all its features") had become frozen into established doctrine. The map prepared by C. F. and E. W. Voegelin (1941)[11] with the colors keyed to Sapir's six divisions was used in training hundreds of students and the matter of the classification of the languages of North America was considered by many to be long since settled. Even as astute a scholar as Kroeber fell under the spell. When material was brought forward in 1958 to suggest that the Algonkian and Muskogean families might be distantly related,[12] Kroeber[13] reacted by declaring, "The overall picture ... is fast becoming chaotic" (p. 19). And then because comparative linguistics had become so firmly associated with classificatory linguistics, Kroeber came even to doubt the value of the comparative method, as shown in the quotation given earlier in the paper.

5. I should therefore like to recommend that we recognize classificatory linguistics as a type of investigation entirely separate from comparative linguistics. In North America comparative linguistics has so far proved very little about genetic relationships beyond the obvious. In the meantime the greatest value of the comparative method has been almost completely lost track of. The separation would also benefit classificatory linguistics since classifiers are so often condemned for making proposals not based on comparative linguistics. After all, classifications have their uses, e.g. as a set of possibly fruitful hypotheses and, prosaically, to give a way of talking about most of the languages of the world without actually listing them. Indeed *most of the languages of the world would have to be labelled unclassified if genetically validated classifications were the only ones that could be used.*

The greatest benefit in the separation, however, should accrue

[10] See a little known note by C. F. Voegelin, "Sapir: insight and rigor", *American Anthropologist*, 44.322-23 (1942).
[11] Published by the American Ethnological Society.
[12] Mary R. Haas, "A new linguistic relationship in North America: Algonkian and the Gulf languages", *Southwestern Journal of Anthropology*, 14.231-64 (1958).
[13] *Op. cit.*

to comparative linguistics. By removing the millstone of classificatory linguistics we could hope to establish a situation where comparative linguistics could be valued in our society for what it is best equipped to deliver instead of being condemned for not delivering something else. Indeed the most devastating thing about classificatory linguistics, at least in North America, is that it insidiously conceals the very areas where comparative linguistics could offer the most by using labelling devices which fail to distinguish widespread families from language isolates.[14] This, I suppose, is part and parcel of a rigorous taxonomy.

In recent papers[15] I have suggested that we use terms which show the rank of protolanguages. Such rankings can be of great aid in clearing up the areas where comparative linguistics can be used most advantageously. Protolanguages of the first order ($PL^1$) are arrived at by the comparison of closely related sister languages, whereas protolanguages of the second order ($PL^2$) are made by comparing two or more $PL^1$s, or a $PL^1$ with one or more language isolates, or a combination of both of these. Language isolates, then, provide no help in unravelling the history of the past 2000-3000 years. They enter in at an earlier stage. On the other hand, sister languages that can be used in reconstructing $PL^1$s conceal a wealth of information only waiting to be revealed by their proper comparison. Over forty per cent of Powell's families are language isolates[16] and therefore useless for that stage of comparative linguistics that we are best equipped to handle.

We need first of all to reconstruct the protolanguages of all true linguistic families (i.e. excluding language isolates). This means the compilation of comparative grammars and dictionaries of Algonkian, Iroquoian, Siouan, Muskogean, Caddoan, Uto-Aztecan, Tanoan, Athapaskan, etc., etc. These would then comprise the

[14]   This unfortunate circumstance goes back to Powell's 1891 classification and is still the most prominent feature of the recent scheme given by Lamb; see Sydney M. Lamb, "Some proposals for linguistic taxonomy", *Anthropological Linguistics*, 1. (2). 33-49 (1959).
[15]   Mary R. Haas, *op. cit.*, and p. 60 of the present volume.
[16]   Mary R. Haas, "Is Kutenai related to Algonkian?", *Canadian Journal of Linguistics*, 10.77-92 (1965); reference is to p. 77.

materials of a series of protolanguages of the first order with a time-depth of 2000-5000 years. These protolanguages could then be compared with each other and with various language isolates in a search for important historical clues. The clues would include: (1) the detection of possible cognates suggesting genetic relationship at a deeper level, (2) the detection of structural similarities also suggestive of relationship, and (3) the detection of possible borrowings showing contact at an earlier period. The great historical significance of borrowings is very frequently overlooked. If they can be shown to be borrowings, they reveal evidence of earlier contact between groups, and in the absence of written history, this can be very significant.

No protolanguage can ever be reconstructed without revealing considerable information about the protoculture at the same time. The earlier kinship system, the numeral system, names of flora and fauna,[17] designations of artifacts — all these will be revealed in some part. More subtle things will also be revealed, e.g. ways of indicating possession, transitivity, and tense or aspect. It is not necessary to go to extremes on any of these points, and in particular it is important to use common sense and ancillary information in drawing both positive and negative conclusions.[18] For example, the fact that it is not possible to reconstruct a single Proto-Algonkian word for 'seven' does not mean that the speakers of the parent language could not count as far as seven; rather the word for 'seven' has been reshaped in the daughter languages and it is not possible to determine which is the reflex of the archetype. There are indeed many hazards for the unwary, but this is no reason for withholding the encouragement of the extensive comparative studies we so badly need in all areas of the world where unwritten languages are found.

---

[17] Frank T. Siebert, Jr., has recently provided an excellent example of this kind of reconstruction for the Algonkian flora and fauna in "The original home of the Proto-Algonquian people", pp. 13-47, in *Contributions to Anthropology: Linguistics*, I (= *National Museum of Canada*, Bull. 214) (Ottawa, 1967).

[18] At one period Indo-Europeanists did go too far in drawing conclusions about the protoculture on the basis of linguistic evidence, and since then the whole area of investigation has been viewed with skepticism in some quarters.

# BIBLIOGRAPHY

Andrade, Manuel J.
  1933-38 "Quileute", pp. 149-292, in *Handbook of American Indian Languages*, Part 3 (Glückstadt-Hamburg-New York).
Barker, M. A. R.
  1964 *Klamath Grammar* (= *UCPL*, 32) (Berkeley and Los Angeles).
Basso, Keith H.
  1968 "The Western Apache classificatory verb system: A formal analysis", *Southwestern Journal of Anthropology*, 24. 252-66.
Bloomfield, Leonard
  1925 "On the sound-system of Central Algonquian", *Lg.*, 1.130-56.
  1933 *Language* (New York).
  1939 "Linguistic aspects of science", *Foundations of the Unity of Science*, 1.4.1-59.
  1946 "Algonquian", in *Linguistic Structures of Native America*, Harry Hoijer and others (= *Viking Fund Publications in Anthropology*, 6) (New York).
  1962 *The Menomini language* (New Haven and London).
Boas, Franz
  1911a "Tsimshian", pp. 283-422, in *Handbook of American Indian Languages*, Part I (= *Bureau of American Ethnology*, Bulletin 40, Part 1) (Washington).
  1911b "Kwakiutl", pp. 423-557, in *Handbook of American Indian Languages*, Part I.
  1920 "The classification of American languages", *American Anthropologist*, n.s., 22.367-376.
  1929 "Classification of American Indian Languages", *Lg.*, 5.1-7.
Boas, Franz and Ella Deloria
  1941 *Dakota grammar* (= *Memoirs of the National Academy of Sciences*, Vol. XXIII, Second Memoir) (Washington).
Bright, Jane O.
  1967 "The phonology of Smith River Athapaskan (Tolowa)", *IJAL*, 30.101-107.
Bright, William
  1957 *The Karok Language* (= *UCPL*, 13) (Berkeley and Los Angeles).
Brinton, Daniel G.
  1892 "The nomenclature and teaching of anthropology", *American Anthropologist*, o.s., 5.263-71.

Cowgill, Warren
1963 "Universals in Indo-European diachronic morphology", in *Universals of Language*, ed. by Joseph H. Greenberg, 91-113 (Cambridge).
Davidson, William, L. W. Elford, and Harry Hoijer
1963 "Athapaskan classificatory verbs", in Harry Hoijer and others (1963).
Dempwolff, Otto
1934 *Vergleichende Lautlehre des Austronesischen Wortschatzes* (Hamburg).
Diebold, A. Richard, Jr.
1964 "A control case for glottochronology", *American Anthropologist*, n.s., 66.987-1006.
Dixon, Roland B. and A. L. Kroeber
1919 "Linguistic families of California", *UCPAAE*, 16.47-118.
Dorsey, James Owen and John R. Swanton
1912 *A dictionary of the Biloxi and Ofo languages* (= *Bureau of American Ethnology*, Bulletin 47) (Washington).
Eliot, John
1663 *The holy Bible, containing the Old Testament and the New* (Cambridge).
Emeneau, Murray B.
1956 "India as a Linguistic Area", *Lg.*, 32.3-16.
1965 *India and Historical Grammar* (= *Annamalai University Publications in Linguistics*, No. 5) (Annamalainagar).
Ferguson, Charles A.
1959 "Diglossia", *Word*, 5.325-340, reprinted in Hymes (1964).
Gallatin, Albert
1836 *A synopsis of the Indian tribes within the United States east of the Rocky Mountains and in the British and Russian possessions in North America* (= *Trans. and Coll. American Antiquarian Society*, II) (Cambridge).
Greenberg, Joseph H.
1950 "Studies in African linguistic classification", *Word*, 6.47-63.
1954 "A quantitative approach to the morphological typology of language", *Method and perspective in anthropology: Papers in honor of Wilson D. Wallis*, ed. by Robert F. Spencer, 192-220 (University of Minnesota Press).
1957 "Genetic relationship among languages", in *Essays in Linguistics* (= *Viking Fund Publications in Anthropology*, 24) (New York).
1960 "The general classification of Central and South American languages", *Selected papers of the 5th International Congress of Anthropological and Ethnological Sciences*, 791-794.
Gudschinsky, Sarah C.
1959 *Proto-Popotecan* (= *Indiana University Publications in Anthropology and Linguistics*, Memoir 15) (Baltimore).
Haas, Mary R.
1941 "The classification of the Muskogean languages", in *Language, culture, and personality*, ed. by Leslie Spier, A. Irving Hallowell, and Stanley S. Newman (Menasha, Wisconsin).
1944 "Men's and women's speech in Koasati", *Lg.*, 20.142-149, reprinted in Hymes (1964).

1946 "A Proto-Muskogean paradigm", *Lg.*, 22.326-32.
1947 "Development of Proto-Muskogean *kʷ", *IJAL*, 13.135-7.
1948 "Classificatory verbs in Muskogee", *IJAL*, 14.244-246.
1950 "The historical development of certain long vowels in Creek", *IJAL*, 16.122-25.
1956 "Natchez and the Muskogean languages", *Lg.*, 32.61-72.
1958a "Algonkian-Ritwan: the end of a controversy", *IJAL*, 24.159-173.
1958b "A new linguistic relationship in North America: Algonkian and the Gulf languages", *Southwestern Journal of Anthropology*, 14.231-64.
1965 "Is Kutenai related to Algonkian?", *Canadian Journal of Linguistics*, 10.77-92.
1966 "Vowels and semivowels in Algonkian", *Lg.*, 42.479-488.
1967 "Language and taxonomy in northwestern California", *American Anthropologist*, 69.358-362.
Hall, Robert A., Jr.
1950 "The Reconstruction of Proto-Romance", *Lg.*, 26.6-27.
Hess, Thomas M.
1966 "Snohomish chameleon morphology", *IJAL*, 32.350-356.
Hockett, C. F.
1948 "Implications of Bloomfield's Algonquian studies", *Lg.*, 24.117-38, reprinted in Hymes (1964).
1957 "Central Algonquian vocabulary: stems in /k-/", *IJAL*, 23.247-68.
Hoenigswald, Henry M.
1960 *Language change and linguistic reconstruction* (Chicago).
Hoijer, Harry
1954 "Some problems of American Indian linguistic research", *UCPL*, 10.3-12.
Hoijer, Harry, and others
1946 *Linguistic structures of native America* (= *VFPA*, 6) (New York).
1963 *Studies in the Athapaskan languages* (= *UCPL*, 29) (Berkeley and Los Angeles).
Howse, Joseph
1844 *A grammar of the Cree language, with which is combined an analysis of the Chippeway dialect* (London).
Hymes, Dell H.
1960 "Lexicostatistics so far", *Current Anthropology*, 1. (1). 3-44.
1964 (ed.), *Language in culture and society* (New York, Evanston, and London).
Jacobs, Melville
1954 "The areal spread of sound features in the languages north of California", pp. 46-56, in *Papers from the Symposium on American Indian Linguistics* (= *UCPL*, 10.1-68) (Berkeley and Los Angeles).
Kiparsky, Paul
1967 "Sonorant clusters in Greek", *Lg.*, 43.619-635.
Kluckhohn, Clyde
1941 "Patterning as exemplified in Navaho culture", in *Language, culture, and personality*, eds. Leslie Spier, A. Irving Hallowell, and Stanley S. Newman (Menasha, Wisconsin).

Kroeber, A. L.
  1916  "Arapaho dialects", *UCPAAE*, 12.3.71-138.
  1939  *Cultural and natural areas of native North America* (Berkeley and Los Angeles).
  1953  Concluding review, in *An appraisal of anthropology today*, ed. by Sol Tax, Loren C. Eiseley, Irving Rouse, and Carl F. Voegelin (Chicago).
  1960  "Statistics, Indo-European, and taxonomy", *Lg.*, 36.1-21, partly reprinted as "The taxonomy of languages and culture" in Hymes (1964).
Kuryłowicz, Jerzy
  1927  "ə Indoeuropéen et *h* Hittite", *Symbolae grammaticae offertes à J. Rozwadowski*, 95-104.
Lacombe, Le Rév. Père Alb.
  1874  *Dictionnaire et grammaire de la langue des Cris* (Montreal).
Lamb, Sydney M.
  1959  "Some proposals for linguistic taxonomy", *Anthropological Linguistics*, 1.(2).33-49.
Lehmann, Winifred P.
  1962  *Historical linguistics* (New York).
Lescarbot, Marc
  1609  *Histoire de la novelle France contenant les navigations, découvertes, et habitations faites par les François* ... (Paris).
Li, Fang-Kuei
  1946  "Chipewyan" in *Linguistic Structures of Native America*, by Harry Hoijer and others (= *VFPA*, 6) (New York).
Longacre, Robert E.
  1957  *Proto-Mixtecan* (= *Indiana University PRCAFL*, Publication 5) (Baltimore).
  1962  "Amplification of Gudschinsky's Proto-Popolocan-Mixtecan", *IJAL*, 28.227-42.
  1966  "On linguistic affinities of Amuzgo", *IJAL*, 32.46-49.
Lounsbury, Floyd G.
  1961  "Iroquois-Cherokee linguistic relations", in *Symposium on Cherokee-Iroquois Culture* (= *BAE*, Bulletin 180) (Washington).
  1964a "A formal account of the Crow- and Omaha-type kinship terminologies", 351-393 in *Explorations in cultural anthropology: essays in honor of George Peter Murdock*, ed. by Ward H. Goodenough (New York).
  1964b "The structural analysis of kinship semantics", 1073-1089 in *Proceedings of the Ninth International Congress of Linguists*, ed. by Horace G. Lunt (London, The Hague, Paris).
Mandelbaum, David G.
  1949  *Selected Writings of Edward Sapir* (Berkeley and Los Angeles).
Meillet, A. and M. Cohen
  1924  *Les langues du monde*[1] (Paris).
Michelson, Truman
  1912  "*Preliminary report on the linguistic classification of Algonquian tribes*", *Annual report of the Bureau of [American] Ethnology*, 1906-07 (Washington, D.C.).

1914   "Two alleged Algonquian languages of California", *American Anthropologist*, n.s., 16.361-367.
Nagel, Ernest
1960   *The structure of science* (New York and Burlingame).
Naish, Constance Mary
1966   "A syntactic study of Tlingit" (unpublished master's thesis).
Oswalt, Robert L.
1966   *Kashaya Texts* (= *UCPL*, 36) (Berkeley and Los Angeles).
Pedersen, Holger
1962   *The discovery of language* (Bloomington). A reprinting of *Linguistic science in the nineteenth century* (Cambridge, 1931).
Pilling, James C.
1891   *Bibliography of the Algonquian languages* (Washington).
Powell, John W.
1891   "Indian linguistic families of America north of Mexico", in *Seventh Annual Report of the Bureau of [American] Ethnology*, 7.7-142 (Washington).
du Pratz, Le Page
1758   *Histoire de la Louisiane*, 3 vols. (Paris).
Pulgram, Ernst
1961   "The nature and use of proto-languages", *Lingua*, 10.18-37.
Radin, Paul
1919   "The genetic relationship of the North American Indian languages", *UCPAAE*, 14 (5).489-502.
Robins, R. H.
1958   *The Yurok language* (= *UCPL*, 15) (Berkeley and Los Angeles).
Salzmann, Zdenek
1950   "A method for analyzing numerical systems", *Word*, 6.78-83.
Sapir, Edward
1909   "Takelma Texts", pp. 1-263 (= *APUM*, 2, no. 1) (Philadelphia).
1913a   "Algonkin *p* and *s* in Cheyenne", *American Anthropologist*, n.s., 15.538-9.
1913b   "Wiyot and Yurok, Algonkin languages of California", *American Anthropologist*, n.s., 15.617-646.
1913-1914   "Southern Paiute and Nahuatl, a study in Uto-Aztekan", Pt. I and Pt. II, *Journal de la Société des Américanistes de Paris*, n.s., 10.379-425 and 11.443-488.
1917   "Linguistic publications of the Bureau of American Ethnology, a general review", *IJAL*, 1.76-81.
1921   *Language* (New York).
1925   "The Hokan affinity of Subtiaba in Nicaragua", *American Anthropologist*, n.s., 27.402-435, 491-527.
1929a   "Central and North American Indian languages", in *Encyclopaedia Britannica*[14], 5.128-141, reprinted in Mandelbaum (1949).
1929b   "The status of linguistics as a science", *Lg.*, 5.207-214.
1931   "The concept of phonetic law as tested in primitive languages by Leonard Bloomfield", 297-306 in *Methods in social science: a case book*, ed. by Stuart A. Rice (Chicago), reprinted in Mandelbaum (1949).

de Saussure, Ferdinand,
1966   *Course in General Linguistics* (New York-Toronto-London), translation of *Cours de linguistique général* (Paris, 1916).
Siebert, Frank T., Jr.
1967a "The original home of the Proto-Algonquian people", pp. 13-47, in
*Contributions to Anthropology: Linguistics I* (= *National Museum of
Canada*, Bulletin 214) (Ottawa).
1967b "Discrepant Consonant Clusters Ending in \*-*k* in Proto-Algonquian",
pp. 48-59, in *Contributions to Anthropology: Linguistics I.*
Silver, Shirley
1966   "The Shasta language" (unpublished doctoral dissertation).
Story, Gillian Lorraine
1966   "A morphological study of Tlingit" (unpublished master's thesis).
Sturtevant, Edgar H.
1939   "The pronoun \*so, \*sā, \*tod and the Indo-Hittite hypothesis", *Lg.*,
15.11-19.
1942   *The Indo-Hittite laryngeals* (Baltimore).
Swadesh, Morris
1959   "Linguistics as an instrument of prehistory", *Southwestern Journal of
Anthropology*, 15.20-35.
1960   "On interhemisphere linguistic connections", 894-924 in *Culture in
history: essays in honor of Paul Radin*, ed. by Stanley Diamond (New
York).
1962   "Linguistic relations across the Bering Strait", *American Anthropologist*, 64.262-291.
Swanton, John R.
1911   *Indian tribes of the lower Mississippi Valley ...* (= *Bureau of American
Ethnology*, Bulletin 43) (Washington).
1924   "The Muskhogean connection of the Natchez language", *IJAL*,
3.46-75.
Teeter, Karl V.
1964a "Wiyot and Yurok: a preliminary study", 192-198 in *Studies in
Californian linguistics*, ed. by William Bright (= *UCPL*, 34) (Berkeley
and Los Angeles).
1964b *The Wiyot Language* (= *UCPL*, 37) (Berkeley and Los Angeles).
Uhlenbeck, C. C.
1927   "Review of A Meillet et M. Cohen, *Les langues du monde ...*, 1924",
*IJAL*, 4.114-116.
Umfreville, Edward
1790   *The present state of the Hudson's Bay* (London).
Voegelin, C. F.
1937-40 *Shawnee Stems and the Jacob P. Dunn Miami Dictionary* (Indianapolis).
1942   "Sapir: insight and rigor", *American Anthropologist*, 44.322-23.
Voegelin, C. F. and Z. S. Harris
1952   "Training in anthropological linguistics", *American Anthropologist*,
54.322-327.

Wagner, Günter
  1933-38 "Yuchi", in *Handbook of American Indian Languages*, Part 3 (Glückstadt-Hamburg-New York).
Watkins, Calvert
  1962 "Remarks on reconstruction and historical linguistic method", in *Indo-European origins of the Celtic verb*, 1-8 (Dublin).
Weinreich, Uriel
  1953 *Languages in Contact* (New York).
  1958 "On the compatibility of genetic relationship and convergent development", *Word*, 14.374-379.
Whitney, William Dwight
  1874 "Indo-European philology and ethnology", *Oriental and linguistic studies*, 1.198-238 (New York).
  1875 *Language and the study of language*[5] (New York).
Whorf, B. L. and G. L. Trager
  1937 "The relationship of Uto-Aztecan and Tanoan", *American Anthropologist*, 39.609-624.

# INDEX

## 118

Massachusetts language, see Natick
Mattole (Athapaskan), 94
Maiduan (Penutian), 82
Mayan, 76
Meillet, A., 111
Menomini (Algonkian), 22n., 25, 29n.,
42n., 43, 44, 67n., 108
metathesis, 36, 37, 38
Miami (Algonkian), 29n., 42n., 43, 85,
88, 89, 113
Miami-Peoria-Illinois (Algonkian),
75n.
Mikasuki (Muskogean), 35n.
Micmac (Algonkian), 66, 75n.
Michelson, Truman, 22, 65n., 66, 111
*Mischsprache* theory, 84
Miwok, Southern Sierra (Miwokan in
Penutian), 82
Miwokan (Penutian), 82
Mixtecan, 50n., 76
morphological change, 51; recon-
struction, 51
Müller, Friedrich, 99n.
Müller, Max, 99
Muskhogean, same as Muskogean
Muskogean, 34, 34n., 35, 40, 43, 44,
46, 52, 59, 61, 62, 76, 81, 82, 90, 92,
95, 96, 105, 106, 109; sound cor-
respondences of, 37
Muskogee, 110; same as Creek
Mutsun (Costanoan in Penutian), 82

Nadene, 85, 86; same as Tlingit-
Haida-Athapaskan
Nagel, Ernst, 33, 33n., 112
Nahuatl (Uto-Aztecan), 26n., 112
Naish, Constance Mary, 85n., 112
nasals, absence of, 89
Natches (language isolate in Gulf),
28n., 49, 61, 61n., 63, 64, 64n., 81,
82, 110, 113
Natick (Algonkian), 21, 29, 66; same
as Massachusetts
Navaho (Athopaskan), 95, 110
Newman, Stanley, 50n., 85
Nisenan (Maiduan in Penutian), 82
Nitinat (Nootkan in Wakashan), 89
Nootka (Nootkan in Wakashan), 89

numeral system, 81, 107

Ofo (extinct) (Siouan), 90n., 91n., 109
Ojibwa (Algonkian), 25, 29n., 42n.,
43, 44, 66, 67n., 68
Omaha (Siouan), 111
onomatopoeia, 82
origin of language, 13
Oswalt, Robert L., 85n., 112
outloans, 48; see also loanwords

paradigmatic sound change, 36, 37
paradigmatic systems, 52; see in-
flectional systems
Passamaquoddy (Algonkian), 29n.,
42n., 43
Pedersen, Holger, 22n., 99, 99n., 104,
112
Penobscot (Algonkian), 29, 42n., 43,
75n.
Penutian, 82, 85, 94, 95
Phonetic correspondences, 33; laws,
16, 27, 112
phonological change, 51; correspondences, 51; diffusion, 84
Pilling, James C., 21n., 25n., 112
Pomoan (in Hokan), 76, 82
Popolocan, 50n.
Popolocan-Mixtecan-Amuzgoan,
50n.
Portuguese (Romance), 31, 66
Powell, John Wesley, 65, 72, 72n., 99,
106, 106n., 112
Powhatan (Algonkian), 29n.
prehistory, 13, 74, 78
du Pratz, Le Page, 28n., 112
prothesis, 27, 39, 43
Proto-Algonkian, 21, 29, 30, 42n., 48,
49, 50, 61n., 66n., 67, 69, 103, 107,
113; see also Algonkian
protoculture, 107
Proto-Germanic, 29, 59, 66; see also
Germanic
Proto-Indo-European, 17, 47, 48, 60;
see also Indo-European
protolanguage, 14, 23, 25, 31-33, 45,
47, 49, 50, 52, 58-60, 63, 66, 75-78,
102, 103, 106, 107, 112; of the first